SELF-CONTROL

POWER TO EXPERIENCE BREAKTHROUGH, TRANSFORMATION AND NEW LIFE

Terri Andres

HARVESTER PUBLISHING
ATLANTA, GEORGIA

Copyright © 2019 by Terri Andres.

All rights reserved. No part of this publication may be reproduced, distributed or transmitted in any form or by any means, including photocopying, recording, or other electronic or mechanical methods, without the prior written permission of the publisher, except in the case of brief quotations embodied in critical reviews and certain other noncommercial uses permitted by copyright law. For permission requests, write to the publisher, addressed "Attention: Permissions Coordinator," at the address below.

Terri Andres/Harvester Publishing
Atlanta, Georgia
harvester-publishing.com

Self-Control / Terri Andres. —1st ed.
ISBN 978-0-578-46270-7

Contents

Author's Note
Preface
Introduction

PART A: *THE WAY* TO BREAKTHROUGH

Your Essentials:
Establishing the Foundation for Breakthrough 34

Your Essentials 2.0:
Penetrating the Heart of the Matter 51

Your Intangibles:
The Superior Unseen Realm and Rule 63

Your Practicals:
Everything You Need To Know To Transform Your Entire Being 84

Your No-Button-Zone:
The Place Where Nothing Bothers You 139

Your Self-In-Action:
Stepping Up Your "A" Game 143

Your Opposites of Good:
Land Mines To Look Out For 161

Your Kit and Caboodle to Start Crushin' It:
Next Level Living 166

Your Greater-Than-Self Perspectives:
Drawing Out Deeper Meaning 178

PART B: *THE WORK* OF TRANSFORMATION

Strategy 1: Accept 191

Strategy 2: Embrace 192

Strategy 3: Examine 193

Strategy 4: Dig 195

Strategy 5: Decide 197

Strategy 6: Edit 198

Strategy 7: Label 199

Strategy 8: Assess 201

Strategy 9: Exercise 202

Strategy 10: Battle 203

Strategy 11: Deny 204
Strategy 12: Endure 205
Strategy 13: Pause 206
Strategy 14: Affirm 207
Strategy 15: Act 208
Strategy 16: Refocus 209
Strategy 17: Identify 210
Strategy 18: Partner 212
Strategy 19: Master 213
Strategy 20: Obsess 215
Strategy 21: Substitute 217
Strategy 22: Immerse 219
Strategy 23: Consume 221
Strategy 24: Jump 223
Strategy 25: Hydrate 225
Strategy 26: Survive 227
Strategy 27: Ration 229
Strategy 28: Fast 231
Strategy 29: Be 232
Strategy 30: Brake 234
Strategy 31: Thank 236
Strategy 32: Speak 238
Strategy 33: Peer 240

Strategy 34: Imagine 242

Strategy 35: Listen 244

Strategy 36: Edify 246

Strategy 37: Read 247

Strategy 38: Coach 249

Strategy 39: Weigh 250

Strategy 40: Slay 251

Strategy 41: Submit 253

Strategy 42: Correct 254

Strategy 43: Detach 257

Strategy 44: Rest 259

Strategy 45: Believe 261

Strategy 46: Anticipate 263

Strategy 47: Forgive 264

Strategy 48: Finish 266

Strategy 49: Expect 267

Strategy 50: Celebrate! 268

PART C: EXPERIENCING *NEW LIFE*

The Purpose of It All:
Understanding The Big Picture 272

Conclusion:
What You Can Look Forward To 275

Bonus Content 278

Appendix 1 280
   12 Sacred Self-Control Truths 280

Appendix 2 282
   Commitment to Mastery 282

Appendix 3 284
   Decisions You Get To Make 284

Appendix 4 285
   A Conversation With Terri 285

Appendix 5 289
   Free Will Confession of Faith 289

Appendix 6 290
   Revelation and Notes 290

Acknowledgments 295

Dedicated to you the reader:
It is my sincere hope that anything – and I pray it is much – you get from what I share here will serve as a catalyst for transformation into the person you see yourself as in order to live the life you see yourself living. For the greater good.

"The secret to success is learning how to use pain and pleasure instead of having pain and pleasure use you. If you do that, you're in control of your life. If you don't, life controls you."

—TONY ROBBINS

AUTHOR'S NOTE

Repetition. Terri has carefully curated any repetition you will find throughout this work. From repeating sentences to seemingly repeating principles. While some principles are in fact similar, they are not entirely the same due to slight nuances in meaning, context and/or practical application.

Research shows, repetitive reading leads to greater learning and recall.

PREFACE

A book entitled *Self-Control* is not exactly what I had in mind for my debut book release.

Frankly, the name is a turn off to many people, is way too blunt and certainly not catchy enough in today's world of book publishing. Big time literary agents would surely skip over it for being too broad and not "nichey" enough for target market business.

If you would have asked me, my first release would have been the 68000-word manuscript about fulfilling your maximum potential I was diligently working on when the inspiration for this book overtook me.

However, when you hear a word from heaven and know for sure that right in the given moment you are under a heavy anointing to *start and finish* a book about self-control in 5 days, you act!

You take massive action and you keep taking it until the project is completed.

So after 12 years of a frustrating pattern of writing and getting side-tracked with various setbacks, this is how my professional writing destiny finally began to come to fruition. In 5 days.

What a powerful demonstration to all of us on the prevailing, perfect plan and timing of God.

But to *you*, dear reader, know that I had *you* in mind while writing this book. I could literally see faces and places of real struggle in this area of self-control. Not only as an imprint in my mind, but in people around me everywhere.

People at work. People at church. People in my community. Friends. Neighbors. Total strangers.

I see with my natural eyes and beyond the struggle for self-control in just about everyone I encounter in a significant way.

The constant battle. And it grieves my heart so much. Which is why I had to write this book.

Terri Andres
July 21, 2019

INTRODUCTION

Within these pages is everything you need to know in order to experience breakthrough; to experience personal transformation; and to experience new life.

To experience a new way of living free from struggle, free from frustration, free from all fear, free from whatever is holding you back in order to start operating at your maximum capacity for creating and contributing to, ultimately, fulfill your purpose and destiny.

Get Back In The Ring

I want you to really hear my heart and what I know for sure: self-control is attainable for you and you can experience breakthrough.

No matter how much you think it is out of your reach. No matter what it feels like right now. No matter how much you have thought or said, *I hate myself* or *I have zero self-control*. No matter how many times you have tried and failed. No matter how many times you have kicked yourself for not sticking to it or staying away from it. No matter how many yells, screams or the river of tears you've cried because of it.

It is not too late to stop some unhealthy habit/behavior and start a new healthy habit/behavior. It does not matter how low or how far you have gone. It is never too late.

> *Self-control is attainable for you and you can experience the breakthrough you desire and/or desperately need.*

You just have to a) have the right knowledge and b) know how to apply it – which is exactly what you will get from reading this book. But first, you must make a decision to not throw in the towel and give up on yourself. Rather, to get back in the ring and fight for it. Fight to become the person you see yourself as.

Every one of us was created with the capacity to exercise self-control. It *is* in you. How can I be sure of this? Answer this simple question: are you or have you ever been a law-abiding citizen? If your answer is yes, you have the capacity to exercise self-control.

A Big Reason Why You Have Not Experienced Breakthrough Yet

I don't have to tell you that exercising self-control to not eat this or drink that or to not do this or not do that is a struggle.

Actually it is a battle. An incessant, moment by moment battle.

But at the core of all our bad habits and misbehaviors, what we are really seeking is to cope and to overcome our struggles with self and the world around us so we can experience true love, acceptance, connection, contentment, healing, health and well-being, happiness, freedom from any form of bondage (including financial debt) and fulfillment from what we contribute to make the world better.

Absent of malicious, calculated evil, the *intended outcome*s of our uncontrolled actions are for some sort of positive result.

We all simply want to exist in a good place. A place of inner and surrounding peace in our lives. We want to be our best. We want to do our best. We want to contribute. We want to feel confident, content and comfortable. We want to love and be loved. We desire peace not perfection. And we want true fulfillment and satisfaction. We also want to feel pleasure and gratification here and there. So we seek to experience all of these things.

Wholeness is what we are really after.

The problem is we go about it the wrong way – which is a big reason breakthrough has not happened yet.

We go about our pursuit for wholeness the wrong way due to lack of right knowledge *and* lack of personal power. Both are key.

What's more – really catch this – is we lack the knowledge of what we should strive to *be* first then what we should strive to *do* as a result of the better person we've *become*. (Read that again)

Right actions come from being right.

Self-control has everything to do with your *being*. Who you are at your core. Your character. From here, actions – right or wrong – come forth.

Equally problematic, we lack the personal power to take consistent, strategic, *right* action against the seen and unseen resistance that incessantly work against us to keep us stuck or self-destructing.

Further, we wrongly believe our good intentions and willpower are enough and altogether miss the third necessity for breakthrough: strategy – which is defined here as a set plan of right (keyword) actions against any and all forms of opposition and resistance.

So we aim with every new year, new month, or new beginning of some sort — with our good intentions and our willpower at the ready — to break through our struggles but inevitably fail. Try again and fail. Try again and fail. Year after year. Try. Fail.

Finding ourselves stuck in a pattern of defeat, we give in to the natural propensities of our lower nature and do what our bodies naturally desire. Whatever feels good — which, unfortunately, is almost always unhealthy and bad — and whatever is fun, easy and/or entertaining.

The "raw feels," as philosophers call it. Bodily pleasures that take little to no cognitive energy. I talk about this in depth in Chapter 4 under the section *Intake* and throughout the book.

About You and Self-Control

Referring back to something I mentioned in the preface, the reason I wasn't thrilled to have a book with the words "Self-Control" in the title as my debut book release is because I understand well the perspective that self-control is not the most appealing subject that people are eager to learn more about and apply to their lives. On the contrary, most people find it repelling.

Acknowledging the need for more self-control is not an easy thing to do.

In fact, most people don't. They don't acknowledge their need for self-control because of pride and/or shame associated with unhealthy habits, indulgences, addictions, or any number of other uncontrolled behaviors. Unless a person is desperate, and hungry and thirsty for more — more freedom, more fulfillment, more virtue — the natural tendency toward admitting the need for self-control is to completely ignore it.

Because of this, a part of me secretly wishes my voice and message was something naturally appealing, and thereby easier to accept and embrace. Something like *How to Be Happier,* or *Unleash Your Creativity,* or *Discover Your Purpose and Passion,* or *Relationship Success,* or *Winning Sales and Marketing,* or *Investing Strategies for Beginners,* or *There's a Leader In You,* or something else "easy."

But it's not. My voice is one you don't necessarily want to hear but *need* to hear — no sugar added!

I am here on this earth to help men and women of all ages, races and classes overcome struggles with self so they can be completely free from frustration in order to reach their maximum potential to ultimately fulfill their purpose.

And what I do know and am absolutely thrilled about is the fact that there are many people who are not repelled by this topic. There are many people — with whom I personally know or have crossed paths with — who readily share their struggles with self-control, their need to overcome and their desire to be their best self in order to live their best life. To become something greater than what they were born as for the greater good of mankind.

I believe you are one of these great people.

Who This Book Is For

To be clear, this book is for anyone who lacks self-control or would like to have more of it, as well as for anyone stuck and need to break free from self-defeating cycles of behavior that stem from excessive consumption of any kind, bad habits, addictions anger, some hurt, crooked thoughts and/or fear to name a few.

Too, this book is for the person who desires to take their self, creativity and productivity in life to the next level and they know having more self-control and mastery over their mind, money, time, relationships and other external factors is exactly what will bridge the gap between where they are to where they want/need to be.

The truth is, self-control (or lack thereof) is something that touches every aspect of our selves and lives.

While you may be struggling to exercise self-control in a particular area, the positive effects of increasing in self-control in that area will begin to show up in other areas of your life.

Such as in your response to an upset spouse or rebellious teenager. Your response as primary caregiver to an elderly and/or ill parent or family member. Your response when your financial institution messed up your last deposit. Your response to a difficult director or coworker. Your response to a new cashier in training when you are in a hurry to check-out. Or your response when you wrongly get cut-off and almost hit by an asinine driver. Whatever it is. More self-control is going to impact you in ways you've never imagined.

What You Can Expect From Reading This Book

From this book you will get revelation knowledge, practical application and a comprehensive understanding of the purpose of self-control.

Specifically, in Part A: *The Way*, I share substantial teaching about self-control and how to experience a breakthrough from anything holding you hostage and stuck in a vicious cycle of self-defeat.

In Part B: *The Way*, I share practical application of self-control through 50 strategies that work to transform your entire being. Strategies – based on physical and spiritual laws and principles, proven scientific research, and personal success – that have completely transformed and continue to elevate my being, life and relationships, as well as the beings, lives and relationships of advance readers of the book. The same can and will happen for you if you apply what you learn in Part A.

Knowledge is indeed power but power does you no good if you don't tap into it.

You have to take action and plug into it. Consider Part B your plugging in.

There is a quote I love by a great 19th century thinker by the name of Thomas Henry Huxley that says, *"The great end to life is not knowledge but action."*

I love this because of its truth. Knowledge is only the beginning. Action is how you are able to keep going and get to the end.

Finally, Part C: *New Life*, is where I wrap everything up with a pretty bow, with the bow representing the big picture, which amounts to the purpose of self-control. I also share the exciting details of how you – your new, powerful, transformed self – can wake up and experience new life every single day and not just the start of a new year, or a new month or a new beginning of some sort but every single day of your waking life.

With respect to reading mechanics, it was important for me to write a book that is content-rich and that packs a real punch. This meant sharing revelation knowledge and research-based information in a direct, in-your-face fashion.

Too, this book is a *simple guide* to self-control and not an academic or psychology book for study. It is absent of all the psychology, scientific and technical jargon that much of what's shared is based on.

Finally, and I hate to say it, but expect to get mad and want to put this book down. Yep. I am 99.9% certain that at some point I will step on a toe or two or maybe even your entire foot.

Many things I share will challenge your current belief system and/or behaviors. But if you stick with me, you will be glad you did.

My main goal is not to get you to agree with me. It is to get you to *consider* with me. To earnestly consider how what I am sharing *could be* true and *could relate* to yourself and/or situation. If we end up agreeing, grand. If not, okay.

> *Just challenge yourself to look for a grain of truth; what could be true.*

Rather than reading something and immediately shooting it down (a natural tendency for most), have an open heart and mind.

Becoming A "Beast" With Strategy

Strategies are intended to bring about specific (keyword) results and by using the word beast I mean becoming prolific in personal strategizing to first *become* and, in turn, behave in a self-controlled manner.

The 50 strategies in Part B are fashioned to facilitate breakthrough — that is, breaking free from something *and* breaking forth to something. Breaking free from and breaking forth to.

As already mentioned, I define strategy here as a set plan of *right* actions against all forms of opposition and resistance — which is not far off from its dictionary definitions.

The New Oxford American dictionary defines it as *a plan of action or policy designed to achieve a major or overall aim.* But, if you that don't already know, this word is also defined within the context of military operations or movements.

The secondary definition is *the art of planning and directing overall military operations and movements in a war or battle.*

Further — and most interesting to me — is strategy is also synonymous with the word *tactic*, another military word that basically means *carefully thought out plans to gain a specific end.*

Now let's really think about this and wrap some context around it.

If your life is extra busy and your goal is to spend more quality time with your family, then you come up with a *plan* for doing so. However...

> *If your goal is to overcome some type of out-of-control behavior and resist that which is resisting you and your life purpose, you better have a strategy to execute when, not if, opposition shows up.*

In the battle for self-control, it is you against yourself. It has been rightly said that self is man's greatest hindrance.

Here is what I really want you to get and brand in your mind: when it comes to self-control you must be strategic.

> *When it comes to self-control you must become very strategic and act strategically 99% of the time.*

If I did not have and keep a strategic mindset – that determines my actions that determines my outcomes – 24/7, I would not have the high level of self-control and mastery I have.

I am always thinking about and acting strategically against evil resistance and the incessantly sensual forces of the world we live in today. By incessantly sensual I mean everything we have at our disposal to instantly engage and gratify any one or all our physical senses – at the same time if we so choose to. (Help, Holy Ghost)

The problem with this – catch what I am saying here – is our physical senses naturally crave what is not good for us and not what is good for us. What do I mean? Very few of you reading this will opt for broccoli or brussel sprouts over pizza or ice cream.

> *To put it plainly, the world we live in is enemy territory.*

As such, I have learned that I must keep a strategic, or tactical, mindset because I realize I am against my own self and if I don't stay on top I will begin to falter. To sink a thousand times faster than took me to reach my current level.

And I am still climbing. Constantly elevating. Never stopping. Never letting my strategic guards down.

The Process of Developing Self-Control

Let me just be frank about this process.

> *Developing self-control is difficult.*

However, this is "the way" that leads to true and lasting (keywords) transformation into your best self in order to live your best life. A life of true love, fulfillment and giving of your time, talent and treasure.

Think of when you are working out trying to lose weight or build muscle. Or practicing becoming an Olympic athlete. Or studying to become a professional so and so. Not one of these feats would come easy. On the contrary, they would all involve some level of pain. The amount of self-sacrifice, self-control, self-discipline, and self-denial for academics, athletes in training, etc is enormous.

However, inherent to the pain, positive transformation is taking place. My point here is to expect that this process will not be easy.

Expect resistance.

Would you agree that in any challenging situation, when you know what to expect you have an advantage? That you gain the upper hand in the situation? Of course.

So now, knowing what to expect, you have an upper hand entering this process of developing or increasing self-control. Expect a little pain in exchange for a lot of gain.

My Hope For You

What I want most for you from reading this book and incorporating the strategies is for you to have life-changing revelations that will lead you to the breakthroughs you need to become your best self.

Regardless of how far away you think you are and how hopeless you might feel right now, you can experience a breakthrough that can lead to a quick 360 degree turnaround for your self and the life you are living. It is possible.

Know that all things are possible for him who believes.

While immersed in this project, on several occasions — because even my own level of self-control went up several notches— I had life-changing revelations that led to breakthroughs, healing and deliverance from things I was aware of but also from something major I was not aware was an issue.

I had not realized the main reason I've never really focused earnestly on having a family of my own is because, while I have a close-knit family and was loved and raised well, there was little nurturing and little emphasis on leaving a family legacy. The focus was on surviving and making ends meet as a result of my parents divorcing while I was still in grade school. The internal brokenness and external circumstances not only influenced but formed the foundation of my adult mentality for family (or lack thereof).

All these years I've believed my lack of enthusiasm for family was solely because I am divinely called to lay down myself in service to others and because of my purpose-driven nature. With this mindset, I chose ministry and the career path instead of marriage and motherhood. I would never try to do both so, for me, I had to pick one or the other.

The point of me sharing this personal testimony is this: When you seek you find. When you ask you receive. When you get serious about your personal development. When you make a decision and commit to that decision.

When you take personal responsibility and do the work to become your highest and best self, breakthroughs and miracles happen.

My Challenge For You

My challenge for you on this journey and beyond is two parts. Come in close to catch these and keep them at the forefront of your mind.

First, to focus more on changing your *self* than changing your circumstances — which is the natural tendency. The biggest problem with focusing on circumstances is, if you succeed at changing your circumstances but don't change your self, you will eventually find yourself back where you started or worse.

When you change, your circumstances begin to change.

Second, to make a decision and commitment to mastery. Mastery of something. Your mind. Your body. Your eating habits. Your input. Your intimacy. Your time. Your talent. Your money. Your emotions or something else. Because what I know for sure is this:

Whether you know it or not or are willing to accept it or not, you are either mastering or being mastered by something.

Decide and commit to incessantly work on some sort of mastery. Why do you think doctors, lawyers, athletes, educators, artists, and anyone who has devoted either their entire lives or most of their lives to mastering something standout, shine, get paid, fulfill their purpose, etc.? It is because of this very reason — their decision, determination and commitment to mastering their thing.

I challenge you to *be* then do the same.

Ground Zero: Belief

I struggled on whether to include this and the very next section on "Truth" here in the introduction or to put them in their own sections because both are so fundamental to change.

I decided to include them here because it is imperative that you *begin* reading this book and *begin* the process of developing self-control with the right context for belief and truth.

Having said this, let me start with a question: do you believe you can have self-control or have more of it?

Know this: you must believe you have the capacity within you to exercise self-control in order to develop it. Why? Because

Your belief system is what determines your will.

Your will to or not to act in a certain way. Sit with this simple yet profound statement until it really sinks in.

If you don't believe you can do something, you are either not going to try to do it or you will try to do it with a weak attempt and will likely fail and give up without ever trying again. On the other hand

If you believe you can do something, all bets are on.

You are going to take action toward your belief and very little – if anything – will be able to stop you from doing what you believe you can do.

No fear. No hater. No naysayer. No negative situation or circumstance. Not even your own self will be able to stop you when you believe.

The etymology of the word belief is *peitho,* a primary verb that has several meanings related to persuasion but the most compelling meaning is to rely on by an *inward certainty;* and from this inward certainty, trusting and having full assurance and confidence.

Now take a moment to think of yourself believing with inward certainty that you have self-control. If you think about this the right way, the very thought should invoke endless possibilities of what you can be and what you can do.

Belief is a powerful force.

It influences and determines your actions (right or wrong) or lack thereof, which then determine your outcomes.

The Game-Changer: Truth

The companion to believing you have self-control is truth. The companion to believing you have self-control is truth.

If you don't believe you have self-control, let me suggest this as a possible reason why: because at some point in your life and various struggles, you bought into the deception that you don't have self-control and never will have it. Consequently, you continue to act without it because this is "just how it is" for you. The hand you've been dealt.

If you can relate, with all due respect, you are deceived if you believe you don't have the capacity to exercise self-control; and it is high time to bust this lie of self-defeat with truth.

The truth is, the capacity for self-control is in you. It just needs to be developed.

If you don't believe you have self-control here is part II of what I think about that: You stopped believing in yourself at some point and resigned to the lie that you don't have self-control and you will never have it because of your past or present failures and shortcomings. And you amplify your belief in this big lie by constantly *telling yourself the story* that you don't have self-control. Hence, uncontrolled actions follow the story.

If this applies to you, here is good news for you:

While acting in a self-controlled manner may not be your present reality, it is not the truth about who you are and what you are capable of.

Together, here in this venue, we are going to further bust this big lie and limiting belief all the way up with truth.

You *do* have self-control within you.

The seed is there. It just needs to be watered and developed through attaining the right knowledge and applying that knowledge to your self and to your actions in strategic ways.

So, get your hopes up! It's about to happen.

Brace yourself for breakthrough.

The Decisions You Now *Get To* Make

Finally, before we dive into Part A, *The Way To Breakthrough*, let me conclude this introduction with presenting you with a couple decisions you, not have to, but *get to* make about the seed of self-control inside of you that is ever ready to grow out of you.

Earnestly consider and answer these two critical questions:

1. Are you *ready and willing* to water the seed of self-control lying dormant within you?
2. Are you ready and willing to *put in the work* that will cause self-control to grow and eventually overcome your biggest areas of struggle and start winning in *every* aspect of your life – areas of struggle and beyond?

The choice is always yours.

If you answered yes to both, keep reading to begin an amazing journey to become your highest and best self and, in turn, live your best life. If you answered no, come back later when you are ready to say *yes*.

Part A: *The Way To Breakthrough*

What You Need To Know To Get You Where You Want To Go

CHAPTER 1

Your Essentials: Establishing the Foundation for Breakthrough

To begin, it will be most helpful for you to have and keep the following *10 Breakthrough Principles* top of mind while reading through Part A.

That you get a revelation of these fundamental truths is imperative to the transformation process so take time to give them earnest thought beyond this initial introduction of them.

Consider this summarized list first, followed by a brief breakdown of each of them:

1. Self is naturally uncontrolled hence our need for self-control.
2. Self-control starts with self-awareness.
3. Self-control is a fruit of acting out of truth.
4. Self-control is a heart issue.
5. Your mental models determine your level of self-control.
6. Your body is your enemy not your friend.

7. Your every action strengthens or weakens your level of self-control.
8. Pleasure weakens you; pain strengthens you.
9. We are not whole on our own so we are constantly striving to *feel* whole over actually *being* whole.
10. Self-control is a personal responsibility.

While not a long list it is an imperative list. Before moving on, read them several times and reflect on them in order to really digest their truth.

BREAKTHROUGH PRINCIPLES BREAKDOWN

1. **Self is naturally uncontrolled hence our need for self-control.** The fact that the act of self-control exists is an indication that self is naturally (keyword) uncontrolled. We *naturally* act uncontrolled and we *naturally* want what is not good for us.
2. **Self-control starts with self-awareness.** Any significant change, personal transformation, starts with awareness of where you are now and where you want/need to be. Awareness is the first step to bridging the gap.
3. **Self-control is a fruit of acting out of truth.** Knowledge of the truth and, more importantly, acceptance of truth is imperative. You must first know your actions are based on some sort of deception. What's more, though, is your willingness to *accept* the truth and decide to act based on it instead. This is challenging for most people because — as the saying goes — the truth hurts. However, you must be willing to course correct in order to increase your self-control.
4. **Self-control is a heart issue.** Simple, but the most profound thought on this subject. Whatever is in your heart is what determines your thoughts and, in turn, your actions

and, in turn, your outcomes. If the desire to exercise self-control exists in your heart *over and above* (key phrase) a desire for some uncontrolled, unhealthy behavior, self-control will win 99% of the time. The remaining 1% is left up for grabs because we are, after all, humans beings made of flesh not stone.

5. **Your mental models determine your level of self-control.** The stories we tell ourselves about any and everything play a huge role in determining our thoughts and, in turn, our actions and outcomes. Said another way, how we think influences our personal power — defined as our ability to take specific and right actions.

6. **Your body is your enemy not your friend.** That your body is your enemy and not your friend is evident. It craves what is not good for it incessantly, and even when it is treated well, it can still decide to betray you with some sickness and disease all on its own with no invitation from you.

7. **Your every action strengthens or weakens your level of self-control.** Every single thing you think and do — everything, nothing left out — has either a positive or negative affect on your being. Think of it like debits and credits that determine the quality of your existence past, present and future.

8. **Pleasure weakens you; pain strengthens you.** This too will challenge most people because the world is so sensual and incessant pleasure is normal. However, the truth is, constantly consuming and partaking in things that give you pleasure weakens your body to whatever you are consuming and partaking in. It starts out "innocently" craving more

but these cravings quickly turn into addictions because our bodies are docile — dangerously docile.

9. **We are not whole on our own so we are constantly striving to *feel* whole over actually *being* whole.** Because we are not whole on our own we constantly do things to make us feel whole. Wholeness is what we are really after, we just go about it the wrong way, *failing to realize whole is a state of being not the way we feel.* We mistake feeling whole from being whole but feeling whole is fake and far from the real thing. Some of the big ways we try to feel whole is by eating, drinking, entertaining ourselves in some way, experiencing some pleasure, keeping ourselves busy, working too much, etc. Whatever the "fix" we choose, we constantly seek sensory gratification. Becoming aware of it and doing the opposite (and even not doing anything and just being) increases our self-control because we train ourselves to just *be* instead of having to do something all the time — something that is usually uncontrolled.

10. **Self-control is a personal responsibility.** It is always up to you and you alone to exercise self-control. Exercising self-control is not only something you *should* do but something you *ought* to do. It should be looked at as being on the same level as becoming your highest and best self — of good moral character, a law-abiding citizen, a good spouse, a good parent, a good neighbor, a good friend, a good worker, etc. Know this: you are responsible for your health, well-being, wholeness and healing. Lack of self-control is responsible for almost every evil, sad or bad thing.

Having these fundamental principles as the frame for everything else shared will do a couple things. One, it will amplify the other thoughts/principles and deepen your understanding to the point of revelation beyond head knowledge. That you get revelation is a big goal.

Two, when you get a revelation of something, right actions tend to follow because, as the saying goes, when you know better you do better. Revelation by itself is in effect useless. It needs to be accompanied with action. Revelation that leads to right actions is the biggest goal here.

The A Factor

Now that we've summarized and understand the overarching principles about self-control here, what's next? The answer is easy. Awareness.

With almost everything, awareness is a major factor. It is a major factor and it is the first factor in the equation. This is especially true when it comes to personal transformation.

Awareness is inherent to change.

You must be aware of something in order to consider, decide, choose, act, react, stay still, improve, etc.

Awareness of *why* your behavior is what it is.

Awareness of your *mindset*. The story you're telling yourself – that is determining your actions – and whether it is based on truth or a based on something that is not truth.

Awareness of your *emotions*. Emotional triggers causing you to act a certain way.

Awareness of how your *environment and surroundings* might be affecting both your mindset and emotions and resulting behavior.

Awareness of how what you are looking at and listening to are affecting your self-control, or lack thereof.

And, lastly here, awareness of how choice of words come into play with your self-control or lack thereof.

At some point, I will go into detail about each of these. Suffice it to say right now, awareness is numero uno in the process of growth and transformation and, in this case, developing and/or increasing in self-control.

Apples To Apples

Before getting too deep – which is coming soon so get ready – I want to make sure we are on the same page in our thinking about various aspects of self-control as used here.

Study these definitions and keep them top of mind as you are reading through the book. These are critical notes for right context.

Self-Control Here Means	Self-control is power over oneself. It is the ability, on a moment by moment basis, to control your impulses and to direct your attention in a goal-directed manner. It will be widely used in this book as simply saying no to yourself (that is, not giving in to and feeding unhealthy cravings and indulgences).
Self-Control is *Vital*	Though this statement may come off as a little bit of an exaggeration, it's not. Self-control is vital. It is vital that we become strong in self-control in order to have optimal health and well-being. Otherwise, we don't thrive and end up living a survival existence and experiencing a poor quality of life because we don't feel well in our bodies. Too, we dramatically increase the likelihood of premature death. Our health is truly our greatest wealth.

Levels of Self-Control	In and of itself, self-control is self-control at the end of the day. However, since we all have unique personalities, are at different stages and phases of life and on different levels in our exercise of self-control, it is going to look different on you than it does on the next person. You may have more or less of it than someone else. Or vice versa. This is all fine as long as each of us are becoming better – our highest and best selves – in our rightful places.
Self-Control versus Self-Discipline	It is important to know the difference between self-control and self-discipline. Think of self-control as your response in a heated situation (in the heat of the moment) and self-discipline as routine (what you do consistently day in and day out). While both are good and profitable, they are not entirely equal in importance. Self-control is far more important because it changes *you* whereas self-discipline changes *what you do*. Self-discipline will start showing up in your life as self-control increases in you.
What Self-Control is Not	Self-control is not something that comes easy. It takes time, it takes conviction, and it takes action and persistence. ***Time.*** You must be patient with yourself and the process. Self-control is not developed overnight. Therefore, you will need to start this journey with a mindset of patience. Which is to say, knowing and expecting highs and lows; not *if* but *when* you fail to keep a commitment or cave under pressure (stress) or due to relentless craving for something you are trying to abstain from.

	Conviction. You must have the will and you have to actually feel passionate when you are not exercising self-control. Passion is conviction. ***Action and Persistence.*** You must have *the works* from your will. Constantly making moves — small but strategic — working your way into fulfilling your maximum capacity for self-control, confidently knowing that it will come to complete fruition at the perfect time for you, your life and where you are in your unique journey to becoming the best version of yourself in your being (body) and in your life (what you do in your body — your thoughts and work of your hands).
Our Key Focus Areas of Self-Control	There are 3 key areas of self-control I will focus on here because these are the areas people struggle in most: 1. Self-control when it comes to Consumption, or Intake. 2. Self-control when it comes to Bad Habits and Addictions. 3. Self-control when it comes to Productivity (purpose and time management).

An Unexpected Necessity

Suffering and glory go hand and hand. Suffering almost always precedes glory and as has been said, the purpose of war is peace.

Accepting your struggle — whatever it is — is necessary for strengthening self-control. Even as counterintuitive as this seems.

First, let me make clear that by this I do not mean being happy about your struggles. That would be offensive.

What I do mean is accepting your battles as opposed to resisting them. The reason why is because your battle is a necessary part of developing self-control.

Hear me on this. There has to be a setting, a situation, by which you (we) who are naturally uncontrolled become controlled. Otherwise there is no opportunity for self-control to abound.

Now is a good time to recall our first breakthrough thought — *self is naturally uncontrolled hence our need for self-control* — while realizing the truth that pain and hardship are inherent parts of growth and maturity.

This thing you are struggling with is working for you not against you.

The purpose of it is for your freedom from it. The purpose of your struggle is for your freedom from it.

Knowing this, a secret to getting through the pain and hardship in the best fashion is to accept it. For the more mature, to go even further and actually *embrace* it, believing and knowing this is actually working for your good!

The big idea here is to go with the wind not against it. Because, the truth is, the more you resist the more difficult you make it on yourself.

So here is my challenge to you: instead of resisting, trying your best not to do this or that, aim to do more of what is right. Focus on doing more of what is right than trying not to do something wrong. Shift your focus on doing more of what is right.

Pause and sit with these thoughts so they can really sink in.

Now, can I break it down a bit further and a bit more real?

What I know for sure is that the struggle you are going through is not meant to break you. It is meant to make you. It is not meant to break you. It is meant to make you.

Your struggle is meant to fortify you.

It is meant to build in you that which is not yet in you but needs to be found in you in order to fulfill your reason for being.

So, do yourself a favor and stop resisting and having a pity-party. These only create frustration and destroy your confidence in your ability to grow. (Read that again)

Right now, *resolve* to stop being angry, depressed, stressed, full of worry, anxiety, shame, guilt and any other self-defeating mindset that is holding you hostage.

The struggles you are going through are meant to make and mold you into the person you need to become in order to fulfill the very purpose for your existence in this life.

By the grace of God, having gotten a revelation of this, I will gladly go through and *grow* through anything that is allowed in my being and life. It is out of my control anyway so why try to fight it? Wouldn't that be foolish? Absolutely.

Hacking Self-Hatred

I know. The last time you tried was supposed to be different. You were determined more than ever before for "this time" to be different. But somehow you've now found yourself right back at square one — or worse.

Over and over and over again you have tried. You have tried everything you know to do and everything someone else recommended you to do.

Mental resets too numerous to count. Practicalities like a Nicorette™ patch or not having the drink, the cookie, the computer or whatever your uncontrolled indulgence is around. But nothing has made the difference you desperately need.

Because of this you have cried a river of tears and have dealt harshly with yourself.

But I want you to really hear my heart here:

This does not have to be how your story continues or how it ends.

You can experience a breakthrough – *if you choose too.*

Listen. The enemy of your soul would love for you to stay feeling self-defeated and hating yourself because of your past and/or present shortcomings.

The lesson to learn here is choosing to separate fact from fiction. And the fact is this:

Failure is an inherent part of any type of success, including developing self-control.

For every success, there are 10 failures that happened before it[1].

Know and accept the truth that in succeeding you are going to fail first. This is just the nature of the process of something becoming something else better.

Think of it in terms of good and evil; hit or miss; win or lose; negative or positive; big or small; hot or cold; succeed or fail; etc.

There is a dichotomy to life where there is always two extreme opposites. And, something to be really excited about, is the fact that self-control is not something you either have or you don't.

Self-control is bred not born.

Armed with this knowledge, make the following simple inner vow to yourself: *Beating myself up for past and/or present shortcomings stops now. No more self-hatred. No more anger. No more shame. I am a work in progress and am succeeding even in any failures that precede my ultimate success.*

Triple Threat C's

These 3 C words are enemies of self-control: Complacency, Comfort and Cravings.

COMPLACENCY

I think of complacency like sleepwalking. A person who is physically awake yet unaware of the important, significant matters of their self, life and purpose — their supreme reason for being born and consisting — or life at-large.

The dictionary definition of complacency is *self-satisfaction especially when accompanied by unawareness of actual dangers or deficiencies.*

Please understand the importance and gravity of this great enemy of your soul and your self-control. The *self* in the self-satisfaction part of the definition sums it up well, as research shows complacency has everything to do with self versus material gain and possessions (anything outside of self).

Really think about that. What this boils down to is this: complacency causes you to actually feel satisfied with *not* fulfilling your maximum potential and ultimately not fulfilling your purpose.

Complacency's negative effect on self-control is that it keeps a person in a perpetual less-than-their-capacity state of thinking and acting that — here's the danger — they are *content* with. Yikes!

Research shows this is either because a) in general, the complacent believe they have already reached their maximum capacity (which is based on their value and belief systems about their self and their ability, whether true or not); or b) they are living life with a victim mentality.

Reflection: *Would you consider yourself complacent?*

COMFORT

Comfort is an enemy of self-control for obvious reasons. When you are comfortable, yes, you stay where you are, but even more detrimental is the *desire* to stay where you are.

Your desire and your will — which prompt your actions— are *working against you* instead of working for you.

With comfort, you are so comfortable (err conditioned) that *you actually resist* any and every slight variation to your feelings of comfort.

You actually resist change because at the first feelings of being uncomfortable as a result of it, you are so uncomfortable that you will go through great lengths to get back to your comfort zone.

Talk about misdirected energy!

Realize this: to resist takes work. To exist in a place of comfort is channeling your energy — *valuable* energy — in the wrong way. Please catch this.

Self-control requires that we not act based on feelings and comfort. It requires our commitment and decisions regardless of how we feel.

Reflection: *Would you consider yourself comfortable?*

CRAVINGS

Brace yourself because this is a big one. All of these are big threats to self-control but this one is really big.

The word craving is another word for appetite.

While studying this out, interestingly, I learned the English word for *appetite* is the same Hebrew word for the soul of man, which is *nephesh*.

With this, the idea that we are our appetites — which is to say, there is no separating the two — can be well-argued.

This means we become what we consume. We literally become what we consume, or take in, and it all started from what we craved and fed the craving consistently.

Wow. I encourage you to read that again so it can really sink in.

Would you like to know what one of the biggest telltale signs for human appetite is? A person's midsection.

In general, our midsections are the most obvious sign of how healthy or unhealthy, controlled or uncontrolled, our cravings and appetites are.

Absent of a causative medical condition, a midsection with anything more than 2x the average girth for their Body Mass Index — to put it plainly, extreme abdominal protrusion — is usually indicative of an OC (out-of-control) appetite for food and/or other consumption.

Now is a good time to recall our simple definition of self-control in the context of cravings: self-control is simply saying no to yourself.

Saying *no* to unhealthy, incessant cravings. Flat-out denying them not feeding them. Putting them to death by starvation.

This is barely the tip of the iceberg. There is so much more to share about our appetites and cravings, which I will cover in a significant level of detail in Chapter 4.

Reflection: Do you feed every craving you have? Is your appetite for food, drink or any other sensory intake healthy, unhealthy or somewhere in the middle?

The Four Big D's

Briefly, the following are four aspects of your personality that play major roles in the formation of self-control, so it is majorly important for you to be aware of them.

DESIRE

This is your passion and represents the core of who you are because your desires flow from what is in your heart. Everything we are (or are not), hope to be, ought to be, etc is a heart issue.

I am sure you have heard the following statement or some flavor of it at some point in your life: *desire determines your intentions, which determine your focus, which determine your actions, which determine your outcomes.*

DECISION

This is your commitment. Your covenant, or agreement, with yourself. Your decisions determine how you show up daily and rise to an occasion. By your decisions, you will be a demonstration of self-control or lack thereof.

DISCIPLINE

This is your sacrifice. Your *yes* to what you ought to do and *no* to what you want to or feel like doing. Your discipline is what you do when you said you would do it even if you no longer want to or feel like doing it.

DIGESTION

This is your intake. What you take in. What you consume through any one of your physical senses. As I just mentioned, you become what you consume. Johann Wolfgang von Goathe put it this way, "we are shaped and fashioned by what we love."

Now would be a good time to go through and complete an informal health assessment to see where your desires are, what your decisions are, what your disciplines are, and what your digestion is currently. There is writing space in the back of the book.

Be brutally honest with yourself. I believe you know that truth must always be the baseline for significant, lasting change.

Motivation

Here is a question for you: what is your motivation for having more self-control?

In general, when it comes to wanting more self-control, most of us are self-motivated. We want more self-control so we can stop doing things we know are bad for us in the long run.

I have good news and bad news about this.

The good news is, this is a *great* reason. One that you should keep.

The bad news is, it's not enough.

As noble as it is, wanting more self-control so you can stop doing things you know are not good for you in the long run is not enough motivation.

If it was enough, you would not be reading this book. You would have mastered self-control a long time ago.

So here's the thing.

An important aspect I learned throughout the process of becoming abundant in self-control is that I needed another reason that was much bigger than little ole me. I needed a greater *why*.

Without a greater why, it was me battling against myself — think good angel on one shoulder and a bad angel on the other. This only created a ton of contention and frustration.

However, when I introduced an external motivating factor that was good, the scale leveled in my favor. I now had my self-motivation *working with* some other external motivation that was also good. More and more, "good" just began to win for me.

In this way, "good" can begin winning for you too.

Having something bigger — something higher, nobler, more significant — outside of yourself along with what you will for yourself increases your strength, your drive, your ability and energy to exercise self-control.

Something bigger strengthens your motivation.

Notes

[1] This is a general statement and not a proven fact based on author research.

CHAPTER 2

Your Essentials 2.0: Penetrating the Heart of the Matter

"*Keep thy heart with all diligence, for out of it are the issues of life*" is the timeless truth and sacred wisdom given to us from the fourth chapter of the Book of Proverbs in the Bible.

Before going any further, I must share the following baseline thought that is central and essential for you to grasp and keep at the forefront of your mind while reading through the rest of the book.

The Baseline

Self-control is a heart issue.

This is a simple statement but is, by far, the most profound thought on this subject. Whatever is in your heart is what determines your thoughts, intentions and, in turn, your actions. If the desire to exercise self-control exists in your heart *over and above* (key phrase) a desire for some uncontrolled, unhealthy behavior, self-control will win 99% of the time. The remaining 1% is left up for grabs because we are, after all, human beings and not robots.

Bible-believing Christian or not, I am willing to bet that, like me and many other people, you have found this ancient proverb to be 100% true. That whatever is in your heart is what determines your thoughts, intentions, actions and ultimately outcomes.

That when you have your heart set on something or bent a certain way, very little, if anything, will prevent you from getting what you want or to bend another way.

The truth that self-control is a heart issue is the baseline for having it in abundance.

When self-control – or anything else for that matter – is in your heart, it is in the most powerful place it can be for it to be activated.

Sure, self-controlled thoughts are great. Sure, willpower is great. Sure, self-control strategies are great and will surely serve you well. But all these pale in comparison to having an unquenchable desire in your heart for the virtue of self-control and, consequently, the application of it in every aspect of your self and life.

This revelation changed me. It moved me from mediocrity to mastery.

My capacity (keyword) for self-control is now through the roof where it will stay as long as it remains a deeply rooted desire and conviction of my heart. I pray the same is or will soon be true for you.

TAKE ACTION

Take a few moments to identify the state of your heart in context here and act accordingly – as you are led or follow my advice here.

If:

- After some examination, you find your desire for self-control is not where you would like or need it to be, ask God to rearrange your heart.
- You feel far away from God and feel like He won't hear your request, thank Him that His grace does not hinge on your feelings. Rather, your faith in Him.
- You don't believe in God, now might be your time to start. There is a *Free Will Confession of Faith* found in Appendix 5.

The Great Exchange

Know this: self-control comes at a high cost. One that, unfortunately, not many people are willing to pay.

The cost of self-sacrifice and self-denial. The cost of saying *no* to yourself and depriving yourself of incessant, temporary instant gratification for long-term, lasting satisfaction and true fulfillment.

Like everything else significant and meaningful you have attained has come at this or another high cost you've had to pay, the same is true for self-control.

For the most meaningful things you have attained, you have no doubt had to sacrifice to get them. Graduating from university. Buying your first house. Paying off mortgage and other debts. Working and serving overtime for the promotions you have gotten.

Self-control is what makes the difference between instant, temporary gratification and long-term, lasting fulfillment. In the short-term, it costs you your sensuality — indulgences of any one of your five senses. However, although the costs are high, the payoffs are even higher.

> ### The link between self-control and self-sacrifice is inseparable.

The more self-sacrifice you have, the more self-control you have. Let me repeat that. The more self-sacrifice you have, the more self-control you have.

If you are going through this life, and there is little to no sacrifice found on some level, with all due respect, you are not operating in your best self or living your best life. Anything worth having is worth sacrificing for. In fact, if it is worth having it is going to *require* sacrifice. This is just the way it is.

> ### The biggest key to exercising self-control is your willingness to not give your self what it wants most of the time.

Imagine me saying this repeatedly with a bullhorn. This is a good mental picture of the magnitude of how vital this principle is. Simply, you have to say *no* to yourself.

The great exchange comes down to your willingness to abstain from what you want and do what you don't want now in order to get what you *truly* (keyword) want later. To get to where you truly desire to be. Not just a quick fix but a lasting felicity of the vision of yourself that you dream about and picture in your mind.

If you are not ready to make the great exchange, it's okay. But you must be honest with yourself. Because, remember, the truth is what liberates. You must tell yourself the truth.

If you have arrived at the point of readiness to make the great exchange —a complete change of heart and mind *and* are willing to say *no* to yourself and suffer through the initial discomfort of self-denial — look expectantly for a shift. Imagine it. Anticipate it. Expect it.

When you do this, I promise you it will show up when these four general elements are present in you: desire, conviction, will and expectation. Note that disgust, desperation and frustration are a few other elements that water the seed of self-control inside of you. You might also have one or a few of these present and pushing you into becoming your destined highest and best self.

The First Big Question

Are you willing to suffer?

Are you willing to suffer through the pain and discomfort you are going to feel when you don't give in to feeding your natural cravings or unnatural addictions?

Two of the biggest hindrances to self-control are pleasure and comfort.

Catch this. People who lack self-control are unwilling to say *no* to pleasuring themselves and unwilling to feel uncomfortable.

But allow me to let you in on a secret. Pain (the opposite of pleasure) and suffering (the opposite of comfort) are better.

Pain and suffering are better than pleasure and comfort.

How? Because — going back to one of our foundational breakthrough thoughts — pleasure weakens while pain strengthens.

For all living creatures, growth and maturation processes are painful. For humans, if you have lived longer than 5 minutes on this planet I am pretty sure you have found this to be true.

So know this. That developing new healthy habits hurt.
- You will experience some physical pain.
- You will feel shitty initially (pardon my French).
- You will experience a lot of resistance.
- You will want to throw in the towel.
- You will feel discouraged, especially before you start seeing results.

But, then, about midway through reaching the initial goal you've set for yourself, the "good and gritty" substance (strength) that has been forming in your character will begin to surface and compel you to keep going and not give up. Again, pain strengthens you.

Personal transformation is indeed difficult and challenging but when you have finally been transformed you are better and beautiful and self-controlled and intentional and significant and purposeful.

The Second Big Question

How much are you willing to suffer?

The extent to which you are willing to suffer is a good indicator into how much self-control you will develop.

The common phrase *no pain no gain* could not be truer.

As I mentioned earlier, there is something about these wonky bodies of ours that want what is bad and doesn't want what is good.

What is good for our body usually doesn't taste good and doesn't make us feel good.

And, in many cases, what is good for us causes us to experience discomfort and, on some level, degrees of pain.

Let's look at fasting for example. Fasting food or fasting sex or fasting entertainment, fasting from talking, or what-have-you.

When you fast from food or sex your body will quickly start yelling at you, *WHAT IN HELL ARE YOU DOING TO ME?!* You will start to feel very uncomfortable. Like you're in hell (I imagine).

The good news is, the discomfort will lessen as time passes. However, it will never completely go away.

The even better news is, the benefits of fasting are many.

First and foremost, you get stronger spiritually.

Physically, you detox your system. Your digestive system gets to rest. You get rid of bloating. You lose inches and pounds depending on how long you fast. You begin the priming process of changing your appetite and cravings and so on.

Mentally, you gain clarity and become sharper. Your mental stamina, or endurance, increases. You become more focused.

The bottom line here is this: exercising self-control — saying *no* to yourself — involves a little suffering. It involves feeling uncomfortable physically and even some mild physical pain depending on your current conditions.

So. What you must settle is, are you willing to suffer?

The Third Big Question

For how long are you willing to suffer?

This is yet another serious question to consider and answer.

The time, or length, in which you are willing to suffer (i.e., sacrifice self) will determine what you are truly seeking.

Here's what I mean.

If all you are looking for is a "right now" breakthrough so you can feel better in the short-term then you will absolutely be able to experience that as you read through this book and begin to apply some of the principles and strategies. Your "suffering" will be short and sweet, so to speak.

However, if you are seeking to be completely transformed and for self-control to become a part of your being versus something you exercise every now and then and especially when you find yourself desperate and hurting because you hit a brick wall. If you want permanent transformation, you must be willing to *live* outside your comfort zone as your way of life. You must say *yes* to constantly sacrificing your self — that is, the lowest, grossest part of your nature that constantly seeks to be gratified — for something higher and greater. Namely, your purpose and service to God and others.

How long you are willing to suffer will also determine how successful you are in achieving stretched goals that requires self-control to endure and stick with it for the long haul.

Ultimately, the capacity for lasting self-control comes down to conditioning (something we will get deep into shortly) and, the longer you practice and train at something, the more conditioned you become.

Also, of huge significance, is the fact that over time the suffering becomes more bearable. Now notice I did not say the suffering gets easier. No, not true at all. Exercising self-control is never something I would call *easy*. Easy is eating the whole gallon of ice cream or drinking the whole pack of beer or bottle of whisky in one sitting.

On an important final note, there is a keyword in these 3 big questions and that is the word *willing*. Your *will*. Your *willingness* to suffer. To feel very uncomfortable because you are not giving in to whatever detrimental demand your being/body is putting on you.

Friend, here is my main point about long-term suffering (which again is self-sacrifice) for the sake of self-control: the longer you endure the more you are able to endure, and this is partly because of your will and partly because of conditioning. I will unpack this thought as we go along so be on the lookout for it.

Why Questions

At some point in the past or as you have been reading up until now, you have probably asked yourself at least one of these four general *why* questions:

WHY IS IT SO IMPORTANT FOR ME TO HAVE SELF-CONTROL?

Frankly, so you can stop hurting yourself. Everything you do — no matter how insignificant it may seem — has either a positive or a negative effect on your spiritual, mental, emotional and physical well-being.

WHY IS SELF-CONTROL SO DIFFICULT?

There are a few reasons. For starters, self-control is not a *natural* propensity of our physical bodies. Our bodies don't *naturally* behave "this way". On the contrary, uncontrolled or out-of-control, is our *natural* behavior.

Ever ate the whole gallon of ice cream in one sitting? Or devoured the entire big bag of chips? Or the whole pizza? Or drank the whole bottle of wine? Eight shots of whisky (like a co-worker of mine recently bragged)? Easily right? Yeah, a-hem, me too. I am so guilty on eating the entire bag of potato chips charge.

While a seed of self-control lies dormant in every one of us, this seed must be cultivated and grown in order to start bearing fruit. And here's the key takeaway: it is each of our personal responsibility to open our eyes to this truth. To become aware — which you are doing now by reading this book — and act in such a way that self-control becomes fully grown and fruitful so every aspect of our being/bodies and lives demonstrate this deeply important maturity.

Too, the other big reason why self-control is so difficult centers around mindset and the stories we tell ourselves in the heat of the moment. And because we tell ourselves these stories (the same story) so much, they become our default mental model — our pattern of thinking — from which our actions stem.

For example, getting out of the bed when you first wake up. What do you tell yourself? Do you say, *just 5 minutes longer*; *this bed feel so good*; *I don't want to get up*. Or do you say, *I cannot wait to get out of bed and get this day started*; *there is nothing for me laying here*; *I am getting up right now because I am excited and eager to work and serve*, etc.?

Your behavior will largely be based on what you tell yourself.

With this, if you need more self-control when it comes to a bad habit or addiction, think about what you are telling yourself in that oh-so-precious moment of decision when you *get to choose* your course of action. Do you say to yourself, *I just gotta have it*; *skip it, it doesn't matter*; *one "last" time won't hurt me* and so on? Or do you say (out loud), *I choose not to do this*; *this is not the best behavior for me to act out*; *this is not what I am truly seeking*, etc.

What I know for sure is that when we use our oh-so- precious moments of decision to pause and actually say out loud something like: *this is not the best decision for me; this is not God's best for me; this is not really what I want to do*, this is a powerful disarming tactic where your actions can and often will follow your words.[1]

There is a wise and true proverb that says

Death and life are in the power of the tongue and those who love it will eat the fruit thereof. (Proverbs 18:21)

WHY DOES IT FEEL SO CRAPPY WHEN WE DENY OURSELVES?

After studying this out from a worldview as well as from a religious view within all the major world religions, the best answer I have come across is the biblical answer: because it is payment for the penalty of sin.

Let me try to break this down succinctly without going deep as this is obviously not the place for it.

Man must pay the penalty for indwelling sin. That is, the sin that lives in us because of the Fall of Man. Sin is sinful. Sin starts out feeling good until you hit bricks or bottom. So, because the flesh of our body is literally sinful, it wants to feel good all the time. So – no surprise – we constantly seek to do things that make it feel good.

Self-control is abstaining from the things that feel good but are not good for us or good for those around us when our actions affect other people. Remember our first, fundamental breakthrough thought: self is naturally uncontrolled. It always wants to be gratified by any means necessary.

WHY DO WE WANT TO EAT WHEN WE ARE NOT SCIENTIFICALLY HUNGRY?

There is a spiritual answer to this as well as a physical answer to this. For the sake of brevity here, I will share the spiritual answer now and share the physical answer in Chapter 4 under the *Appetite* section.

The over-simplified spiritual answer is because we are not whole creatures in these wonky, ruined physical bodies and, consequently, we incessantly seek to *feel* whole. Not *be* whole (which should be the pursuit) but feel whole. Food makes us feel *like* we are whole.

The moment our flesh is no longer gratified, we feel uncomfortable and when we eat — or consume/engage in other indulgence — it makes our flesh feel comfortable and whole-*like* again.

But the catch is our flesh only feels "whole" for a short time for the duration of the comfort activity and maybe, if you're lucky, a little while longer after you're done.

Can somebody say temporary fix? Can somebody else say vicious, unhealthy cycle of self-sabotage?

I unpack this in Chapter 4 under the *Patches* section but here the key takeaway reduces to default human body behavior when it comes to self-control — or lack thereof.

Once again, it is appropriate to refer back to our first fundamental breakthrough thought: *self is naturally uncontrolled hence our need for it.*

Notes

[1] Of course, there are some other elements that need to be present like your desire, conviction and will to not go there.

CHAPTER 3

Your Intangibles: The Superior Unseen Realm and Rule

The things you cannot see but are far superior than the things you can see.

In this critical chapter I will cover intangibles that impact self-control. These include your spirit/soul, your mind/thoughts, your feelings/emotions, your personality, your character, and, last but certainly not least, the unseen forces that resist you in exercising self-control.

Mind Matters

As you may already know, there is a lot to the connection between self-control and our minds. (Fair warning, this section on the mind is longer than others. I have broken it into subsections to make it easier to follow and, hopefully, keep your interest high.)

The first earnest thought I want to share is this: don't make self-control harder than it has to be by thinking too much. I cannot fully articulate how important this seemingly simple thought is.

So exactly what do I mean?

I mean don't meditate on the things you are "missing out" on. Instead, direct your thoughts to say focused on what is right in front of you.

If you don't focus on what is in front of you and instead overthink, think ahead and meditate on that thing you could be indulging in, you are only going to hinder your development of self-control. You are also going to make the process a lot more difficult.

What your mental striving should be is to focus on how the process and temporary discomfort you are experiencing is going to have a really big payday sooner or later.

So what would this look like practically?

If you are abstaining from an unhealthy guilty pleasure (fried chicken for example), don't constantly think about it to the point that your mouth is watering and you can literally taste it. Keep your mind focused on something else. The more meaningful that something else is the better.

If you are working, be laser focused on your work and when (not if) your mind begins to stray, quickly snap back.

If you are not working or doing anything in particular, focus your thoughts on savoring a memorable experience or anticipating a new one. Or start reading or researching something of interest.

Now is a good time to remember one of our fundamental breakthrough thoughts: *your mental models — the stories you tell yourself — determine your level of self-control.*

Self-control is largely mental.

Long before writing this book, I always said self-discipline starts in the mind. This is also true for its first cousin self-control. If you can get your mind right, your actions will be right.

This is a widely known, proven scientific fact. That the way we think determines our actions. We know this part well.

What we don't realize, consider and act from are the facts that our minds are *easily* deceived, *easily* tormented by fear and phobias and *naturally* doubts.

Why is this significant? Simply because we end up thinking the wrong thoughts. Rather than our thoughts (ultimately, actions) being based on truth, our thoughts are based on things that are not true.

Because of these mental hindrances, we don't think about things in the right way. How can we? We can't until we come into the knowledge of truth.

Truth and only the truth liberates.

It liberates us from any and everything but in the context we are discussing here, it liberates us from thinking unhealthy habits, consumption and uncontrolled behaviors are okay. Once we realize and accept they are not, we are able to change direction and travel down the right path that leads us to self-control.

Once our thinking is aligned with truth — right thinking — right actions will follow.

Finally on this, know that changing the way you think is a process. Most often a long and, unfortunately, painful process (like it was for me). But for some of you, this will not be the case. For some of you reading this, you will be at the end of a painful journey and will be able to readily receive the revelations being shared here.

Whichever of these apply to you, be encouraged and trust that you are right where you should be for your unique journey.

(I encourage you to pause to digest what I've shared so far. Perhaps even read everything up to this point a second time before moving on as these are big, challenging truths I just dropped)

SELF-CONTROL AND THINKING OUTSIDE OF OURSELVES

Continuing on *Mind Matters*, one of the most beneficial, transformational-for-the-better things I have learned to do is train my mind to view people and situations from lenses outside of my own. Rather, to look at what is happening to me or what is happening around me from different perspectives.

Now, I know this sounds pretty elementary but for the average person it is not an easy thing to do and, what's more, to do it consistently.

To do this — particularly when someone has deeply upset or offended you or a loved one — takes an above average mastery of our natural thought processes of hatred, anger, unforgiveness, retaliation, revenge and division/separation.

Naturally, our minds don't work right.

Our minds are bent certain ways based on our DNA, how we were reared, our experiences, the environment/culture in which we were raised and what we witnessed. And, unfortunately, it is the ill experiences from the latter two of this list that stick with us and shape our thinking and responses. We remember the bad, not by choice, but because it messes us up.

So be keenly conscious of this from this point forward.

Begin to start training your mind to look at situations from a perspective outside of your own if you've had bad experiences.

What would this look like? If you are in an awkward situation with someone, look at it from their perspective *above your own*. If you are in a disagreement with a spouse or boss or neighbor, friend or family member, look at it from their perspective *above your own*.

Most importantly, look at the situation from God's perspective and not a merely human perspective. If you do this, it will serve you well in so many ways all the days of your life.

OUR DESIRES AFFECT OUR LEVEL OF SELF-CONTROL

Something else significant that also determine our mindset toward self-control is our desires.

What we think about and dream about constantly, we will eventually act out. So, the critical piece to assess is if your desires cause your actions to be controlled or uncontrolled.

Pause now and think about your dominant (keyword) desires. You will notice your actions are aligned with them.

BEYOND DESIRE: IMAGINATIONS THAT MAKE OR BREAK YOUR SELF-CONTROL

On one hand, our imaginations are powerful tools at our disposable, but on the other hand they can be dangerous tools at our disposal.

A powerful tool in the sense of overcoming an area of struggle with visions of victory and overcoming. As a man thinks in his heart so is he.

A dangerous tool in the sense of how prone we are to creating stories about things, people and situations that are only true in our mind/imagination because we desire them to be. We, in effect, become disillusioned by our own desires. We see only what we want to see. Can someone say *dan-ger-rous*?

> *In this sense, fear has the same effect on our mind as desire does.*

Irrational fear also creates stories in our mind that are only true in our mind. We not only see what we fear but that's all we see because it becomes big and overwhelming in our minds. So what *seems* true in reality is not.

Here is the key takeaway: our desires and fears disillusion us and it takes self-control not to allow our minds to go here. I like the way Joyce Meyer put it. "Where the mind goes, the man follows."

SELF-CONTROL PREVENTS DISILLUSIONMENT

Ladies and gentlemen don't get it confused — a crush is a crush. It doesn't mean you are soul mates and destined for marriage.

I learned this — as I am sure many of you have as well — when I had the biggest crush on a guy and in my own mind made it out to be something it was not.

When reality struck, my gut reaction was to blame him for leading me on but looking back there was no leading me on. He was innocent and every bit of it was the result of the story I repeatedly told myself about him and "us" for months. #PersonalResponsibility

We do this because desire, particularly selfish desire, is that powerful and seducing.

We write the entire story in our mind and someone would be very hard-pressed to tell us otherwise. Because, not only did we write the entire story in our mind, but we wrote the story and we've played it and over and over and over and over and over and over and over and over and over and over and over and over in our mind until something happens to snap us out of our fantasy back to reality. Hear me: it takes self-control to not do this!

Any discipline starts in the mind so when it comes to self-control, make sure your mindset is not crooked.

THE PARADIGM SHIFT IN OUR THINKING

For self-control, we need a complete paradigm shift in our thinking and, particularly, as it relates to our physical bodies.

We need to accept and embrace the truth that our bodies are not made for what we have come to use and abuse them for: endless pleasures, instant gratifications and fixes of any and every kind.

I know this is challenging and will no doubt be a hard pill to swallow for many of you but, (ahem) with all due respect, your rejection of truth does not phase *truth*.

As I mentioned earlier and well worth mentioning over and over, one of the most leveling things I have learned to do is to view things outside of my own perspective. *#Humility*

First, from the perspective of Almighty God. Second, from the perspective of the other person, people or whatever entity/institution involved and last through the lens of my own perspective.

Why is this such a game-changer?

Because our own perspectives are naturally defensive. They are laced with fear. They are laced with offense. They are laced with biases from our upbringing, experiences, hurts, and our selfish desires.

Ouch.

> *Now is a good time to call to mind that truth liberates.*

Emotional Intelligence

Question: Why do we need to be emotional intelligent?

Answer: because of stress and the many stresses we must deal with and effectively manage in order to live and thrive in our world today.

Human behavior stems from the mental and emotional states an individual is in. With this, suffice it to say, controlling our emotions is of critical importance.

> *Our emotions, aka our feelings, play an enormous part in our level of self-control.*

When we are in heightened emotional states like being extremely upset, exhausted, hungry and even being rude, offensive or the like to someone else, our capacity to exercise self-control decreases a great deal.

When we have reached these and other ill states, our amygdala (a tiny mass in our brains that has the big job of managing our emotional responses) immediately reacts and wants out – if I can put it plain. It immediately wants to be and feel and experience calm and comfort as quick as possible.

So, rather automatically, we look for the first instant gratification we can get ahold of. Think "comfort food," for example.

Further, there are all kinds of emotional triggers we face daily: personal and professional stress, worry, anxiety, fear, depression, loneliness/isolation, illness, frustration over finances, family issues and loss of some sort.

Because of all of these, we must be intentional (not automatic) in how we respond.

> *We must go all-against our natural tendencies. <u>All against</u> them.*

Pause for reflection: *what would it look like for you to go all-against your normal reaction to someone or something that pushes your buttons?*

When we are emotionally intelligent, we have developed the ability to well-manage (*well* being the keyword) our feelings when life hits.

> *The emotionally intelligent remain calm and remain in control.*

Emotional Intelligence (EI) is a fairly recent, rising and fascinating area of scientific study. Psychologist Daniel Goleman popularized its ideas in his best-selling book *Emotional Intelligence: Why it can matter more than IQ* back in the mid-1990s. EI is a way of understanding the emotions of ourselves and others and learning to control these emotions so that you can choose what you say and what you do, in order to engender the outcome you would like to see.

> "The key difference between someone who uses EI and someone who does not" writes psychotherapist and life coach, Christine Wilding, "is that the emotionally intelligent person will fight to maintain control of their emotions and refuse to allow them to dictate their actions unless appropriate. The person who is not using EI will simply give sway to the emotions, regardless of the out-

come (and then, of course, say 'I couldn't help it. It just happened')"[1]

If I had to guess, stress (mental and/or emotional strain), hurt and addiction are probably the top 3 reasons why people don't exercise self-control.

Finances, in particular, cause major emotional (and often physical) stress thus are a major trigger that acts against self-control. When we are in a state of frustration, the natural reaction of our chemistry is to want to feel better ASAP. This is because being in a state of frustration is not how were designed to be.

Frustration is not what we were designed for, so naturally we want to eliminate the frustration and do whatever will make us feel better. So we find the quickest raw feel and we feast on that. Our chemistry was made to exist in peace and experience love, joy peace and happiness,

As I have mentioned several times now, we are all just trying to make it. Just trying to cope and get through life's struggles.

Stress is a large part of living and earnest stress management skills are needed by all of us. However most people don't have the awareness — I wrote this book to help change this — they need to manage stress to the extent that it needs to be managed. Consequently, they do what is fun, easy and entertaining, again, as an escape just trying to cope and feel better.

The key takeaway here is stress is a major trigger for uncontrolled and out-of-control behavior and if we can manage our stress to the point of minimizing it, or better yet, keeping it at bay, we will exercise more self-control by default. Because, what I believe is, we all want to be our best and do our best. We really do. It is just a matter of having the personal power to make it a reality 100% or as close as possible to 100% of the time.

Are you with me? Super.

Self-Control Suckers

Having just spent a good amount of time on triggers that cause you to act against self-control, it will be helpful for memorization and recall to show all the major triggers separately here in table form.

Anger	Brokenness	Depression
Fatigue	Finances	Frustration
Hunger	Hurt	Loneliness
Loss	Rejection	Sadness
Self-Indulgence	Sickness	Physical Pain

Table A: Major triggers that cause you to act against self-control

Stuck In Feelings

Something I have observed with others and something that was certainly true of myself for many years is, most people are stuck in their feelings.

Which is to say, what they do or don't do is based solely on how they feel and nothing else.

In addition to always going after raw feels, their *perspectives* are always from the position of how they feel. Their *actions* always stem from how they feel and their *interactions* with others are all based on how they were made to feel by that other person, group of people, institution and/or organization.

Too, when it comes to something as great as *inspiration*, we love to be inspired. Little do we know, there's a catch.

"Being inspired" is not the most accurate description of what is really going on most of the time when it comes to "being inspired."

What is more accurate of the powerful dynamic at work here is

> *Most people love to _feel_ inspired. Not be inspired, but merely feel inspired.*

They love to hear inspiration within their own interests. They love to read and watch inspiration within their interests. They fill (feel) up until they are overflowing with waterfalls and rivers of inspiration.

However – really catch this – being inspired carries a connotation of *doing something* as a result of your being – in this case being inspired. In other words, inspired action should ensue.

Sadly, most never get to the doing.

Most people stay stuck in feeling inspired to the point of addiction to it and never get around to doing what they have been inspired to do. I call this *inspiration addiction*.

I know what I am sharing here is 100 because I am sharing from personal experience.

For years (15+), I was stuck feeling inspired but never moving beyond my feelings to take any significant action. I would start something but would never finish it. I was addicted to the feeling.

I had the sense of purpose. I had the vision. I had the conviction. I had the will. I had the motivation. I had the commitment and in most cases had the knowledge. But even being equipped with all these, I lacked the absolute essential: *personal power*.

Personal power is your ability to take action — consistent, massive action – and keep taking it until your goal is accomplished.

Lacking personal power can be due to many things. Missing one, several or all the elements from my list above; being burdened down by stress; financial duress; bad habits; bondages/addictions and, of course, lack of self-control.

Confidence also makes the cut and is one of the two particular areas of lack that severely hindered my personal power. (The other area was procrastination, both of which, along with personal power, I will go into detail about in the following two chapters.)

In this context, lack of confidence and self-control run neck and neck in the detriment department by sharing a common attribute: *weakness*.

When you lack confidence, you feel like your weaknesses are bigger than your strengths. When you lack self-control, you make feeling pleasure (which ultimately weakens you) bigger than saying *no* to yourself (which ultimately strengthens you).

So, the important question is, what can we do about this?

The simple answer is to keep your feelings in check. Stick with the truth and stick with the facts in order to take consistent, strategic action.

Self-control enables you to take action regardless.

- *Regardless* of how you feel.
- *Regardless* of whether you feel inspired or motivated.
- *Regardless* of what is or is not happening to you or what is or is not happening around you.
- *Regardless* of your situation or circumstances.
- *Regardless* of fear.
- *Regardless* of insecurity.
- *Regardless* of intimidations.
- *Regardless* of what you see.
- *Regardless*... (you fill in the blank)

Gaining mastery over your self strengthens you to move beyond flaky feelings to act solidly and accordingly in order to achieve your desired outcomes.

The G Factor

"Man's greatest hindrance is self" *Unknown*

The G factor is the god factor.

The Book of Psalms[2] in the bible teaches men are gods, made a little lower than the angels. The idea being, as gods, we were created to rule, reign, have dominion and live in complete freedom.

You might be asking rule, reign, and have dominion over what and for what?

The answer is over *self* for the purpose of *creating*.

Man was made to create and creating requires self-control.

It takes self-control to engage and fully immerse yourself in the creative process. Once you've reached this point, creating then works to actually increase self-control.

Realize this, that so much of our uncontrolled or out-of-control behavior is simply because we are lacking more constructive use of our time. Let me repeat that. So much of our uncontrolled behavior is just because we are lacking more constructive use of our time.

Think about it.

When you are really into doing something, creating something significant, you are into it. Laser-focused on the task at hand and laser-focused on finishing. And, if it is a passion project, you become engrossed and you do not want to be interrupted.

Remember this next time you find yourself frustrated and flustered and feeling the urge to indulge in something unhealthy. *As soon as you feel the urge* — this is your moment of opportunity, your oh-so-precious moment of decision — start creating something. Write, draw, paint, create some content, record music, develop something, sing, do whatever is creative.

Can you now see how creativity increases self-control?

When you are in control of yourself versus self controlling you, you are free to be, create and do anything.

As you increase in self-control your G factor, your godliness, will increase.

I am convinced that man is most like God when we behave like gods and are in complete control of our selves.

Since we're on the subject, let me leave you with a God-thought to consider.

While I have just encouraged you to behave like a god and self-control being a fruit of doing so, by virtue and definition of what a god is, there can only be one god operating in your life.

A god is a supreme being and supreme is supreme. It is singular not plural thus there can only be one God/god ruling over you and directing your decisions and actions. So it is either you as your god or God as your God. It can never, at any time, be both. It must be one or the other.

Pause for reflection: *what is true for me and my life currently, and how is this working for me?*

Using Your Words

"A man's belly shall be satisfied with the fruit of his mouth; and with the increase of his lips shall he be filled." Proverbs 18:20

Chances are you have heard this before, or something like it that conveys the importance and power of your words.

How words have creative power. How words are things (according to the wisdom of the late and great Dr. Maya Angelou). How words have the power to determine how you feel, your actions and so on.

All of these are good and I personally have found them to be true. What I want you to realize here is the connection between words and self-control. It is an important one.

First, words are energy and energy is a source of life. Energy energizes. It enlivens. It empowers you to move. With this, we can rightly conclude that your words have a *major* effect on your actions.

> *Every word you speak – because of the energy that is created from them – will have either a positive or negative effect on you and, in turn, your level of self-control.*

Speaking words that edify and encourage will carry positive energy and speaking words that deconstruct and doubt will carry negative energy.

Words also paint pictures that help shape your mental models — which are your beliefs, ideas, images, descriptions, etc. of how something works. Your experiences are what largely determine your mental models but so do your words.

If you, like most of us, have ever had someone say something so hurtful to you that it not only jaded you but, consequently, it also affected your interaction with other people, then you know the truth of how words have a profound effect on us. Probably the most common, or relatable, example of this is found in a romantic relationship situation where either you said or had something hurtful said to you.

The key thing to remember is *every* (no hyperbole here) word you speak, read and hear has a positive or negative impact on your mindset, energy and actions. And, because of the laws of Physics, you can be sure that there is always an outcome associated with energy. Good energy. Good outcome. Bad energy. Bad outcome.

This is great news because we get to control our outcomes.

It all comes down to what we choose. Moment by moment choices that we get to make that shape our moment by moment experiences and outcomes. Please don't miss what I am conveying here.

The connection words and affirmations have with self-control is it takes self-control to establish a routine (keyword) whereby you do this.

When God told me to use my words to change my world *every day,* He also whispered that it would take self-control for me to do it; but if I did it, I would change my world.

This rocked me because it was a divine word from heaven that I was ripe and ready to receive and act on.

I started out strong but unfortunately wasn't strong enough. I don't remember exactly how long I went but I got off track within that same month.

What happened?

My level of self-control wasn't strong enough. My issue — which God knew — has always been finishing what I start.

The One who knows the end from the beginning knew I didn't have enough self-control to do this. This is the very reason why He told me to do it. To create an opportunity for me to become aware, adjust and improve. To create an opportunity where I could build my self-control when it comes to using my words in the form of daily affirmations.

The fruit that has been produced from this is now I finish what I start and now I use my words to change my world every single day.

And so can you. Boom. [Fist bump]

Up-play Affirmations

Most people don't know the power of affirmations.

Aside from largely being looked upon as being a bit hokey, affirmations promise so much yet when it comes to achieving authentic, lasting results, for most people they fall short.

I, on the other hand, have found otherwise. I have found that affirmations are absolutely powerful and can absolutely change your life, as well as *instantly change your mental state* – which is a pretty big deal. Wouldn't you agree?

Affirmations are a great tool to have in your self-control toolbox when you find yourself in a heat-of-the-moment type situation.

The keys to affirmations are your belief, your consistency and your timing.

First and foremost is actually believing what you are affirming. Second, declaring your affirmations at a set time every day and especially in the midst of defining and challenging moments.

Moments when you feel weak like you can't go on.

Moments when you feel so much anger that you could be a beautiful darker skin-toned individual whose color changes to beet red.

Moments where you just gotta have this or that and if you don't you feel like you are going to lose it.

In these moments, affirm yourself. Affirm yourself with words of truth.

Tell yourself speaking out loud with power and authority: *I am strong. I am strong. I am strong. I believe in myself. I believe in myself. I believe in myself. I am full of power. I am full of power. I am full of power. I am in control. I am in control. I am in control. My self, my circumstances and no other person controls me. My self, my circumstances or no other person controls me. My self, my circumstances or no other person influences negative reactions and actions from me...*

Speaking each affirmation more than once is important. Repetition will increase the positive response from your body's central and peripheral nervous systems.

Whatever your struggle is, self-control and otherwise, tell yourself the positive opposite. Even if you don't believe what you are saying yet.

The power is in your speak.

I think that is worth repeating. Even if you don't believe what you are saying yet, it is ok because there is power and influence in your speak. There is power and influence in utterance.

The words you speak are full of unseen energy. Negative speak, negative energy. Positive speak, positive energy.

Pretty elementary right? Yet difficult for most to not doubt and do on a consistent basis in heat-of-the-moment situations as well as in normal day-to-day experiences that have a way of pushing the right buttons. Like traffic. A difficult boss or co-worker. A rebellious teenager. A needy friend or relative. A relationship on the rocks. A financial crisis.

Starting today, challenge yourself to be persistent and consistent in affirmations and you will begin to see a turnaround.

Your actions follow your words.

This is what you must know and bear in mind when you don't yet believe what you are saying yourself.

Here are a few more self-affirming examples:
- I am in control of myself and I have self-control in abundance.
- I am in control of my emotions.
- I am in control of my temper.
- I am in control what I say.
- I am in control of my finances and spending.
- I am in control my habits and am replacing bad habits with good ones.
- I am in control my thoughts; my thoughts do not control me.
- I am in control of my body; my body does not control me.

CC & GC

For the sake of privacy, I won't reveal their names, but CC & GC are two amazing women I aspire to be like in one way or another.

When I need to exercise self-control in a given moment and am not particularly feeling like doing so for no good reason or am legitimately feeling too weak for whatever reason, I think about one of their excellent examples and wanting to elevate myself to their level and beyond.

I ask myself, what would CC say or not say in this situation? What would her posture be? How would GC think about this situation? What would she do, how would she do it and when?

Muses are very powerful influences on us.

We can be motivated by others that inspire each part of our being — spirit, soul and body.

The definition of muse *is a woman, or force personified as a woman, who is the source of inspiration for a creative artist.*

When you are in the process of developing or increasing self-control, you are definitely going to need some inspiration at times. So spend some time thinking about what or who truly inspires you to be better and why. Then when it comes time for you to exercise self-control and you really need to press-in to do so, you'll have some help.

Notes

[1] Wilding, Christine. Improve Your Emotional Intelligence. The McGraw-Hill Companies, Inc. 2013. Page 5

[2] See Psalms 8:5 and 82:6

CHAPTER 4

Your Practicals: Everything You Need To Know To Transform Your Entire Being

As the chapter title indicates, what I will be sharing here is powerful practical knowledge. Expect many, if not all, of your *how do I* questions in the context of self-control and your total being (spirit, soul and body) to be answered.

You can also expect to read – and hopefully receive – revelation knowledge, which would simply and loosely be defined as ideas and perspectives that are new to you and, moreover, resonate with you and changes how you see something.

So, without further ado, let's get into these powerful practical's for developing and increasing self-control.

DISCLAIMER: it is about to get real and a little raw at times, so brace yourself. Know everything I am sharing is from a place of respect and sincere concern for your health and well-being. My purpose here and in life is to help you become your best.

Real Wealth

My aim here is to impart revelation. Albeit brief, this *Real Wealth* section has potential to transform your entire physical being (body) so come in close and comprehend with your spiritual eyes and ears.

Here is the key principle: *your real wealth is your health and a major factor for how healthy your physical body is not necessarily your weight but rather your waistline.*

> *Your overall health can largely be determined by the size of your midsection.*

By its girth (i.e., width, thickness, wideness, bulk) and by how it feels regularly based on how your digestive system is functioning.

Before really unpacking this, go with me here to get a better picture of my point. Imagine you are about to cook some type of meat for breakfast lunch, dinner or what-have-you. Steak, chicken, bacon, pork chops, sausage or something else. As a part of preparing to cook the meat, you will inspect and clean the meat if necessary. You will also remove excess fat (the visible white stuff that is a bit gross looking on raw meat. It doesn't look as bad when cooked). You proceed to remove the fat because you know it has zero benefit. It looks bad, tastes bad, has a bad texture and, in fact, is bad for your health. You instinctively know that eating fat like this is not only unhealthy but harmful if consistently consumed in significant amounts.

But wait. Let's step back and really think about this. You trim fat from meat before cooking it so you won't ingest it, yet you regularly ingest foods and food ingredients that turn into fat that is mostly stored in your midsection (waist). Or, more accurately said, stored around your body's vital organs.

Does this make good sense? Is it intelligent? Is it wise?
Let's keep going.

As I am sure you know, your abdomen houses most of your digestive system (stomach, small and large intestines (colon) and two of your five vital organs (kidneys and liver).

Study this diagram of the inside of an abdomen.

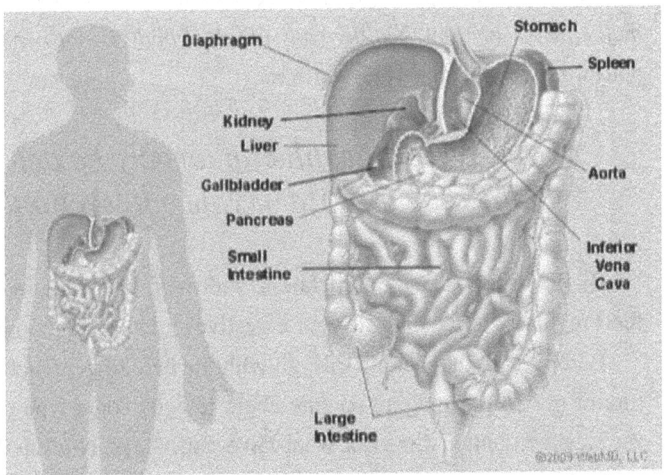

Now study this picture of the outside of an abdomen[1].

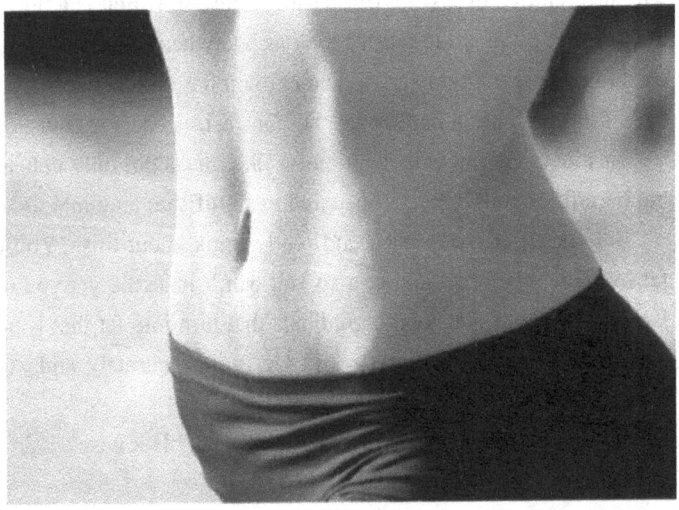

What, if anything, stands out to you in these two images? What I notice that is most significant to our context is there is nothing extra on the inside causing severe protrusion on the outside. Everything on the inside is supposed to be there and has a specific function, and there is nothing foreign or fatty there that is not supposed to be there.

Here is the challenging truth: outside of medical causation, in no place should your abdomen be severely protruding outward.

Severely being the keyword. There should be no *severe* protrusion in the upper region, in the lower region, on the left side or on the right side[2].

Now, am I suggesting you should have no belly fat and a flat abdomen that looks like this picture? Emphatically, no! Having some belly fat is actually beneficial in more ways than one — as long as it is the benign kind of subcutaneous fat (think love handles) and not the more malignant kind of visceral fat that becomes embedded deep within your abdominal parts causing inflammation and metabolic syndrome that are the root causes of sickness and disease.

But here's the thing. Our modern culture and society has effectively deceived masses and convinced us that "love handles" and "beer bellies" and a big stomach from "good eating" and middle-age midsection bulge is to be expected as you age. However, I am here to tell you the truth: *these conditions are not normal and not ok for optimal health and well-being. The truth is they are harmful to your health and well-being and often an obvious indication of the presence of sickness and/or disease.*

Do you see this truth? More importantly, *will you accept* this truth? Marinate on this for a while before moving on.

LET'S INTERACT

Now I would like to engage you in a couple key ways.

First, I want you to pause and ponder your digestive system for a few moments Think about how well it functions. Ask and answer these questions:

1. Do I feel well or do I feel like crap most of the time?
2. Does my midsection feel uncomfortable?
3. Do I eat on an empty stomach or a full stomach so when I actually feel full already but I am not able to control myself enough to refrain from eating?
4. Does my food digest easily or do I have indigestion most of the time?
5. Do I have regular bowel movements?
6. Are my bowel movements "complete" where it feels like everything came out?
7. Does my stomach feel upset most of the time?
8. Do I have to strain a lot to get the waste out?
9. Does my digestive system feel clean I begin eating my next meal or does it still feel completely full or even partially full, etc.?

These are just a few general questions. I encourage you to ask your own questions because you know yourself better than anyone. When you ask the right questions, you get the right answers!

Second, ponder your waistline for the next few moments[3]. Look down at it. Go to a mirror if you have to in order to really set your gaze and get a good look.

Is your waistline much bigger than what it should be? Ideally, for men, your waistline girth should measure no more than 40 inches. Women, yours should not measure more than 35 inches.

Do this quick and easy exercise (if you will but no pressure). Now or whenever convenient, grab a tape measure and measure your waistline girth. Simply wrap the tape loosely around your waist at your belly button.

Is your waistline a whole lot bigger than what it should be? If it is, ask yourself why and answer honestly. Consider if it is because of a medical condition. Or because of what you have been ingesting? Overeating perhaps?

What I mean by overeating is consuming so much that your digestive system is not able to digest what you've consuming fast enough so therefore excess food and whatever else you've consumed end up storing in and around your abdominal organs?

Finally here, a point worth mentioning is how so many people mistake their abdomen for their stomach. When you put your hand over your abdomen and think or say, "my stomach is hurting," this may or may not be true. More than likely your stomach is not really what is hurting because your stomach is located in the upper left region of your abdomen (right beneath your heart) not in the bottom of your abdomen – the area people touch and rub for "stomach aches" Turn back to the diagram to see what I am talking about.

Now, I am certainly not a medical doctor – so none of what I am sharing should be interpreted as medical advising. I am also not saying people never have real stomach aches. Of course we do. I am merely pointing out this common misconception.

Going back to belly bulge, if you have *severe* midsection protrusion, it is likely visceral fat is the blame. It is important for you to realize fat is salty and causes inflammation — the root of all disease. Fat also causes blood vessels to burst (which causes pain that could be mistaken as a "stomachache") and a host of other ills.

Vital organs surrounded by fat is not an ideal environment for them to thrive.

At this point, some of what I have shared might be ringing true for you and you might be asking yourself, *so now what*?

What is my first practical step to real wealth now that I've learned some new truths and accept them as true?

Without question, there are many other things you will need to become educated on in terms of dietary intake, and, as you continue on this path of being more self-controlled, you will start having the revelations that will bring about certain awareness that will lead you to the right knowledge (truth). The universe will see to it.

But for right here and right now, my best advice for traveling the road that ends in real wealth is this: with all due respect, kindness and genuine concern for your optimal health and well-being

You must stop consuming so much.

Which means getting your appetite (keyword) for food and drink under control. Which is what we will dive into next.

DISCLAIMER: all this being said, I am not a qualified physician and you should not take what I am sharing as medical advice or instruction. I am simply sharing knowledge of what I have read, researched and, in cases, experientially found to be true in these areas.

Appetite

This whole idea of appetite is such a large subject that I could (and likely will one day) write an entire book on it.

Let me start with a request. I ask that you open your heart and mind to really catch what I am about to share.

Be *graciously considerate* of these thoughts in that you are slow to take offense. Many things are going to challenge your mindsets and behaviors. Know my intention is never to offend or make you feel bad, but rather to share life-changing and liberating truths that lead to better being, better health and better well-being; which beget a better quality of life for yourself, your life and your loved ones.

RAW FEELS

We all have an appetite as a part of our makeup as human beings and there are two aspects of human appetite — spiritual appetite and physical appetite. Make sure you get this: *two* aspects of appetite.

At our core, deep within, what we truly yearn for is spiritual fulfillment and satisfaction. But, due to lack of awareness of this, natural instincts and conditioning (based on whatever our consistent intake is), we are constantly trying to fill this *spiritual desire* (err void) with physical gratifications that don't cut the cake, never can and never will. So we end up starving our spiritual appetites and, consequently, unknowingly exist in a state of spiritual depravity.

But here's the big thought to catch – just because our spiritual appetites are deprived does not mean they die.

Your spiritual appetite will never go away as long as you are physically alive because you are a spirit being with a spiritual appetite. Your spirit is the superior part of your triune being of spirit, soul and body.

The great contention with our spiritual and physical appetites is they oppose each other.

Both appetites constantly hunger to be fed and we must wisely choose which one to feed and when. Our hunger for spiritual meat is the deeper and greater one because our spirit is the superior part of our being. If it is never, rarely or barely fed, our innate survival instincts will naturally act to fill this void with some sort of physical "feel." *Raw feel* as philosophers put it. Does this make sense? If not, re-read this section as many times as necessary until it sinks in.

MAKING IT PERSONAL: YOUR APPETITE

Just with the little I have shared so far, pause and take a moment to ponder your own appetite. Were you aware of the existence of your superior, spiritual appetite? If so, how well-fed is your spiritual appetite compared to your physical appetite? Are you in control of your physical appetite or does it control you?

If your spiritual appetite is starving because your physical appetite is the only one being fed, your human beingness is gravely imbalanced. Grave because our appetites and actions that stem from them are one of the key things that determine the quality of our life moment by moment. Read that again then catch this revelation:

There is a significant difference between scientific hunger and appetite.

Scientific hunger is the *need* to feed your body with food. It has an element of suffering to it in that your body literally begins to feel weak and uncomfortable when you are truly hungry. Scientific hunger is where your body is severely lacking food.

Scientific hunger, interestingly, is also easily satisfied. Have you ever truly been hungry — on the level of starving with the presence of hunger pangs and all — then ate the smallest morsel of food and almost instantly the suffering of hunger and hunger pangs you were feeling seconds before subsides?

In this scenario, scientific hunger was satisfied almost instantaneously on contact. So, why is it that in our world today, we are hard-pressed to go more than 1-3 hours without eating something? And when I say eating, let it be stated for the record, we are eating way, way, way more than small morsels.

The answer is because of our physical appetites.

Appetite, on the other hand from scientific hunger, is first and foremost all about the *desire* for something. Within context here, the desire would be for food or some other physical intake.

Secondly, appetite is where your cravings come from and — catch this — you are most hungry for what you feed on and what you focus on. The more you feed on something, obviously the more you crave it.

When you are seeking to exercise self-control in an area of struggle related to these, ask yourself if you have a legitimate need or is it merely desire. Also consider this thought from *The Science of Being Well* by Wallace D. Wattles: "in eating, man must learn to be guided by his hunger. He must distinguish between hunger and appetite, and between hunger and the cravings of habit; he must NEVER eat unless he feels an EARNED hunger."[4]

CRAVINGS:
SCRATCHING THE SURFACE

Let's step further into cravings. There is deeper revelation I want you to lay ahold of here.

The dictionary definition of a craving is *a powerful desire for something*. This is a pretty simple definition for such a significant force of energy that could either be very good or very bad depending on the craving and how often it is catered to.

Power and *desire* are the two keywords about cravings.

Power is defined as a) *having great power or strength; b) having a strong effect on people's feelings or thoughts*. Desire - a) *a strong feeling of wanting to have something or wishing for something to happen;* b) *strong sexual feeling or appetite*.

Ah ok. Now we are getting to the heart of cravings.

We are starting to see how our cravings are linked to our feelings which are linked to our urges and appetites (food, drink, sexual and otherwise).

There is a significant body of scientific research around cravings. Some studies suggest that our bodies are actually built to crave as part of a survival tactic during times of famine.

Then, at the opposite end of science, there is the spiritual aspect of cravings to consider which is largely determined from what gets through the gateways to our souls – which are our eyes and ears.

The etymology of the word *craving* is the same word as soul - nephesh, which I find to be very interesting. The implication being:

1. Cravings are connected to the state of your soul
    a. The state of your mind
    b. The state of your will
    c. The state of your emotions (feelings)
2. You are your cravings
    a. Your person and your cravings are one in the same
    b. What you are craving is a reflection of who you are

Pause for reflection. Are you having revelations? What connections are you making?

CRAVINGS: A DEEPER DIVE

With all this talk about what cravings are, you might be wondering *why*? Why do we crave incessantly and what we can do to control them?

There are two aspects to cravings. The spiritual aspect and the physical/physiological aspect. Before sharing details about both, let me start by sharing this powerful truth and most important thought:

We crave constantly because are constantly seeking to feel whole.

We crave constantly because, ultimately, we are trying to feel (keyword) whole. As I have expressed a few times now, wholeness is what we are really after and we try to reach wholeness through our feelings by feeding cravings. Read that again.

The sneaky thing about feeding our natural cravings is, while it seems so and feels so, they can never make us whole.

Cravings interfere with our pursuit for true soul satisfaction. Wholeness is an inside job – spiritual – and cravings are a part of our physical appetites and gratified with things such as excessive food consumption, sugar, caffeine, nicotine, narcotics, sex and other artificial stimulants including sensational news feeds, images, videos, other digital media – all of which are *temporary* raw feels; which is why you have to constantly fill (err feel) up on them.

Consider this interesting etymological word study that reveals the intertwined nature/relationship between you and your cravings.

> The ancient Hebrew word for craving traces back to the word appetite and the word appetite is — get this — the same word as the word soul, *nephesh*, which is defined in all the following ways: *self, life, creature, person, appetite, mind, living being, desire, emotion, passion, that which breathes, the man himself, seat of the appetites, seat of emotions and passions, activity of mind, activity of will and activity of character.*

Finally, with respect to the physiological aspect of cravings, here are 3 scientific summary points to keep in mind about them:
1. These cravings are associated with and stem from our mind, or neurological processes.
2. These cravings are associated with and stem from our mood, or emotional state.

3. These cravings are associated with and stem from our memory, or chemical satisfaction stored in our sensory memory[5]

Mind, mood and memory are the 3 M's behind the physiological aspect of cravings. All three being solely physical states (mental, emotional and sensory).

Given all this, is it still any wonder why your cravings are for whatever will trigger the highly sought dopamine hormone that is produced during such activities as sex, compulsive gambling, doing some type of drug or consuming fatty and sugary foods and drinks?

What is more though is realizing you and I get to determine and control the cravings of our bodies based on how we manage these three states.

HOW TO HANDLE CRAVINGS

Know that you are always going to have cravings. Cravings are never going to go away. Because, as the word study revealed, cravings are connected to your appetite which is one and the same with your soul.

Since cravings are here to stay, in the context of increasing self-control, our focus must be effectively managing them.

The best thing I have learned to do for keeping unhealthy and harmful cravings in check is to feed on – no *devour* – healthy, wholesome, profitable things in order to condition (keyword) my natural cravings to crave healthy versus unhealthy.

This is the most effective approach because your cravings are the result of what you consume consistently. I repeat, your cravings are the result of what you consume. Whatever you feed your body; it wants more of. Said another way, you have in effect conditioned your body in a certain way and from whence the craving(s) will come. The cadence is consume, condition, crave. Consume, condition, crave. Consume, condition, crave.

> *The craving is your body's incessant demand on its condition – how you have conditioned it over a significant period of time.*

We all have conditioned our bodies to determine what they crave. However, there is good news. Though difficult, cravings can be resisted through willpower. Remember, they are partly governed by our minds.

Here is a quick, simple, powerful and effective 1-2-3 step to resist a craving by sheer willpower (using food as the example):

1. **Acknowledge it.** Acknowledge that you are just having a craving and that you are not really scientifically hungry.
2. **Speak to it.** Talk back to it and tell it *no! You are an unhealthy, ill craving that can ultimately lead to premature death and I do not have to feed you.*
3. **Deprive it.** Instead of feeding the unhealthy craving, there are two routes you can go for this third step:
    a. Feed on something else healthy.
    b. Not feeding the craving and redirecting your attention and energy to something creative and constructive.

> *Constructive activity kills nagging cravings.*

This is a form of transmutation, which is the complete transferring or transformation from one state to another.

When you are craving and have the strength not to give in to it in that moment, that is good, but it is only a start. You must do something else with that energy, otherwise there is a good chance you will give in to the craving sooner or later – usually sooner. Like very soon (within minutes) after you've resisted.

Unless you do something with that energy. Either choosing better or choosing different.

So here is my advice. Based on what your top 3 personality strengths are (find out what they are at strengthsfinder.com), do something constructive that, ideally, utilizes one of your top strengths.

Or, choose to work on your passion project (I'll talk more about this later). Or, connect with a friend or a loved one in a significant, meaningful and authentic way – in person or over the phone.

All of these are effective ways to diffuse an unhealthy craving.

CRAVINGS AND YOUR ENERGY LEVEL

Another key thought about appetite is the more you feed its unhealthy cravings, the less zeal and energy you have.

Let me repeat that. The more you feed unhealthy cravings, the less zeal and energy you have.

Unhealthy cravings are raw feels — whatever feels good, tastes good and looks good. And now is a good time to recall part of one of our fundamental thoughts: pleasure weakens. Pleasure weakens and de-energizes you.

Stating the obvious, weak is the opposite of strong. And when you are weak, you lack energy. Energy is power and strength.

Every time you indulge in whatever your pleasure is, you get weaker and weaker.

What is interesting is, while you physically get weaker and weaker, the craving gets stronger. This is bad because it is unhealthy!

What's worse is, once habit forms, you will look up and, tragically, find yourself caught in the addictive grip of a poison that disguised itself as a pleasure.

Smoking a cigarette gives you an artificial shot of energy (if you can even call it that) while you are smoking and for a few minutes after, but the long-term effect is dependence on this artificial stimulant for "energy." Then you'll need to smoke again. And again. And again, until now you depend on 1-3 packs for your daily physical exertion.

The same with alcohol. Poison disguised as a pleasure. The same with prescription and illegal drugs. The same with promiscuous sex. The same with pornography. The same with overeating.

All unhealthy cravings that are poisons disguised as pleasures.

THE CONCLUSION
ON APPETITE AND CRAVINGS

With all of the above being said, I want your key takeaway to be this: You are your appetite. You are your appetite: You cannot separate yourself from your appetite.

You are literally what you eat. You are what you take in. What you consume. *And,* how often you consume it. Just like you become like who you are around. You become like what you consume.

Why is this so significant? Because intake is *everything*.

It plays a large role in determining how you think and, in turn, how you behave. Your intake impacts your thoughts and actions.

In the Introduction, when introducing the idea of *raw feels*, I shared how, at the end of the day, we are just trying to cope with the struggles of life and we just want to be happy and have inner peace and outer circumstances, but the problem is we go about it the wrong way — absent of truth, wise judgment and strategy — and in doing so we end up amplifying our struggles.

This is because these raw feels (ecstasy, thrills, orgasm, delight, mirth, exuberance and comfort), while extremely and immediately satisfying while engaged in them only last for as long as you are engaged. If you're lucky, up to a few hours afterward.

Needless to say, we easily get hooked on these things because of the way they make us feel physically, mentally and emotionally. After all, the loose scientific definition of happiness is positive emotion.

Do you see the problem with all of this? Any happiness and/or satisfaction from raw feel pleasure is short-term and not lasting. What's worse is we become addicted to what only lasts short-term and not truly fulfilling in the least bit. Hence, we find ourselves in a vicious cycle of feel-good, frustration, feel-good, frustration, feel-good, frustration and so on.

I hope by now you are seeing how everything about this is negative and it all stems from physical appetite and cravings.

There is a popular saying "change your thoughts, change your life." This is a very true statement. Let me submit another very true statement that you won't hear much in these days where self-control is so lacking and abhorred:

> *"Change your APPETITE, change your being, change your life."*

Intake

Piggybacking on several of the concepts from the previous section on *Appetite,* your intake, or what you consume, is everything when it comes down to self-control.

How so? Because it is what determines your cravings which, next to the thoughts of your mind, is the most powerful driving force for your actions. Read this over and over and over again until the truth of it resonates.

The word *consume* has several definitions:
    a.   To eat, drink or ingest
    b.   To use up
    c.   To completely destroy
    d.   To absorb all of the attention and energy of someone

The word itself is from Latin *consumere. Con* meaning altogether and *Sumere* meaning take up. So, *consume* means to altogether take up. To altogether take up.

Think about that.

Whatever it is that you consume, your body — your being — is altogether taking it up. Whatever you consume, you are altogether taking it up.

Simply put, you become it and it becomes you. Said another way

> *What you consistently consume, ultimately consumes you.*

Pause for reflection. Has the little bit I've shared about intake been a big revelation for you? I sure do hope so but let's continue.

It is important for me to point out that what we consume is much more than food — which is typically the first thought when thinking about consumption. Our intake includes food, drink and anything we ingest through our physical bodies. But it also includes what we look at. What we hear. What we touch (intimacy with people and otherwise) and what we smell.

Think 5 senses. Any sensory input can be considered as your intake.

Now is a good time to remember that you are becoming what you are consuming. Self becomes what it consumes.

An important nuance for you to catch about intake is the fact that what goes in *does not* just go out. The popular phrase "garbage in, garbage out" does not apply in this context.

As human beings, what we consume, we absorb. That is, actually becomes a part of us.

Said another way, what we consume literally affects the matter of our material make-up — all the way down to a molecular level.

Really think about this.

You can be Hungry Jack™ hungry with legitimate earned hunger where you have labored and burned significant calories but can eat the smallest morsel of food and literally be satisfied in terms of that fierce hunger instantly subsiding. Have you ever been here?

This is because as soon as that substance (in this case food) hit your bloodstream — catch this — it became a part of you and your body instantly began to go through the digestion process.

Another example. When a drug addict takes a hit of whatever, they experience a high *instantly*. Why? Again, absorption. It begins on contact with the bloodstream.

Finally, food allergies are another very good example of this type of on-contact absorption.

My point spelled out if you can't clearly see it by now is this – exactly what I started out saying: we become what we consume.

Intake is a big deal.

Pause for reflection. Before reading any further, take time to give earnest thought to what you have been consuming and, consequently, what and/or who you have become as a result.

DEEPER REVELATION ABOUT INTAKE AND SELF-CONTROL: ANSWERING WHY?

So now the question to consider is, why is intake (consumption) such an important revelation to have as it relates to self-control?

Here's why

In the world we live in today — with the dark sides of technology at our fingertips — you are going to be taken out if you do not control what you are taking in.

Let me repeat that. In the world we live in today — with the dark sides of technology at our fingertips — you are going to be taken out if you do not control what you are taking in, particularly through your eye and ear gates. What comes through these channels of our senses form us. Shapes us. Makes us and will eventually overcome us – in a good way or bad way.

I can hear you asking, *how so*?

Because of what I've already shared about absorption. Our soul absorbs our consumption, and this is *the how* of the truth that whatever we are consume literally becomes a part of our material selves.

Just like our bodies absorb the tangible food and drink it receives, so too do our souls absorb the intangible things it receives.

If your soul is constantly vexed, consider your intake.

When you watch scary movies 24/7, you will inevitably have scary images replay in your mind and scary dreams. Likewise, if you watch romantic movies, you will inevitably have romantic images replay in your mind and romantic dreams. And, unfortunately, the same is true for XXX movies. You will inevitably have these types images replay in your mind and dream about them.

If you are consistently listening to gossip and negativity all the time, you will inevitably begin to gossip and be negative in your speak and, in turn, your actions.

Finally, this is a good time for me to remind you that pleasure weakens while pain strengthens. If you are feeling pleasure most of the time by consuming that which is sensual every chance you get, you will be weak in self-control. However, if, on the other hand, you want self-control to the point where you can taste it — some real power operating within your self and life — then you've got to pull back on all your pleasures and be willing to suffer a little bit for it.

To not have the donut. The potato chips. The pizza. The ice-cream. The cigarette. The sex. The porn. The fix. The hit. The hamburger. The shot of whiskey or shot of whatever. The _____ (you fill in the blank).

You have to be willing to tell yourself no and be willing to suffer through the initial uncomfortable feelings you are going to feel when you don't feed the unhealthy cravings of your current appetite.

This is just how it works. And the choice is always yours.

All of this may have you feeling a bit discouraged. Don't be. There is good news. You can change unhealthy appetites and cravings with conditioning, which I go over a few sections from here.

Feed Responsibly™

Catch this: Everything sold is not meant to be consumed.

There are tons of extremely hazardous-to-your health "food" stocked on supermarket shelves today masked as harmless through compelling marketing and enticing packaging.

True story. One day while strolling through a Meijer grocery store, I found myself starting to head down the liquor aisle. When I peered down looking on both sides of the aisle, I saw nothing but bottles of liquor of different shapes, shades and sizes. What was most astounding to me was the fact that the entire aisle was filled to capacity. Now, if you have ever shopped at Meijer you know this is a big box, 1-stop retailer that is larger than other average-sized big box stores. It is like a Costco. This was a very long aisle jam-packed with bottles of booze. I was astounded by the volume of it.

Never before (and not now) ever casting judgment on people who choose to drink – as I was swiftly moving to turn my cart around – I said softly to myself *this is the poison aisle*. This comment took me completely by surprise because, again, I had never felt any kind of negative judgment toward alcohol and the people who drink it. Intrigued, not long after that when I got home and settled, I looked up the etymology of the word *intoxication* and found it related to the word *poison*; concluding that, when someone becomes intoxicated they've poisoned their body — which immediately lets them know it has been poisoned and is now in protection/recovery mode when it starts to vomit the poison out. Well, well, well...

My gut instinct (the *poison* comment) that day in Meijer was right and I only share this, not to cast judgment or make you feel bad for drinking[6], but because I was reminded of this as I write about consuming things that, while readily available and widespread, are not beneficial and in many cases are harmful to you.

Getting back on topic – feeding responsibly – let me try to very simply break down the unfortunate "food" reality of today:

- There is "food" everywhere that is not real food that is hazardous for your health.
- There is "food" being sold not because its nutritious and necessary to sustain life, but only being sold for money in some INC's, LLC's or sole proprietor's pockets.
- Multitudes of millions of people continuing to, quite literally, feed on and thus financially support this evil, money scandal.

Where is the win? Where is the win for you the consumer? There isn't one. Not only isn't there a win, there is loss. Loss of optimal physical and mental health and well-being being the biggest.

The next question is *why*? Why do consumers continue to be a part of this insanity?

There are 3 top reasons:
1. Lack of knowledge of the truth
2. The insatiable desire to feel good
3. Sugar addiction

If you are going to reach success in self-control, it is vital that you know better and thus do better when it comes to your food consumption.

First, be conscious. When you are feeling stressed, know that your body is just looking for relief and calm. Know that you have the power to choose healthy, satisfying options. Awareness is key.

Get this. Scientific research from the National Institute of Health has proven that superfoods are actually better than comfort foods when it comes combating stress.[7] They nourish and detoxify our cells *and also* produce "feel good" neurotransmitters serotonin and dopamine. Oatmeal will produce serotonin in the brain just like cookies and ice-cream will. Spinach and other leafy greens will produce dopamine just like heroin, crack or cocaine would.

Second, commit to educating yourself on how to *Feed Responsibly*™. Feeding responsibly encompasses these: to eat responsibly; to drink responsibly; to look responsibly; to listen responsibly; to touch (in terms of intimacy) responsibly; to anything you consume responsibly[8]. It is absolutely true that knowledge is indeed power and when you know better you usually tend to do better.

Third, un-prioritize food. Understand that you will never get to where you desire to be if you keep giving food such a big place in your being and life.

> *For far too many, food has too big of a place in their being and lives. Mostly everything revolves around it.*

It comes before creating and being productive. Before beneficial religious and spiritual practices and disciplines. Before studying. Before many important things. Food, unfortunately, has become one of our biggest idols.

I know people – and more than likely, you do too – who get downright *mean and mad* when they do not eat. They become absolutely no good until they get some grub. Do we need to eat? Of course we do. But we need to eat to live not live to eat.

Finally, you must simply say *no* and resist the temptation to treat your body/stomach as a dumping ground and stop nearly gorging yourself because of the raw, sensational gratification garbage food is intentionally manufactured to give you and to addict you. #*Money*

Ouch. I know these truths might hurt if the shoe fits. Please be forgiving and know I write this with love, respect, compassion, and a sincere desire for you to be well and live your best life.

The Unseen Factor

Above I touched on how the stress component of feeding responsibly is often what triggers unhealthy, out-of-control behavior. While this is certainly true, there is something deeper for you to grasp.

I refer to it as the unseen factor.

Know this, that the typical situational/circumstantial stressors of your life are the mere inferior elements at work (although it may not seem or feel like it). The more superior working is our psychological outlook.

Our mental perceptions and emotional states are not only determining our actions but also our physical conditions as well; the actual health of our bodies.

What we think and the way we think has a profound effect on our physical behaviors — which of course includes eating and all other consumption.

Really listen to me here and take note. If you have a bunch of bitterness, biases, anger, unforgiveness, hurt and hatred in your heart – all of which are unseen – these are the biggest factors determining unwanted actions and outcomes within your self and your life. These and other negative, energetic ills ultimately result in mental and physical sickness and disease of varying kinds from varying causes. Meditate on this a bit before moving on.

Here's what to do about it: pray. Soul search. Look within. Examine *your self.* Pause from blaming. This is about you and God and no one else. Ask for His help to heal your hurt and trust Him to do what only He can and wants to do for you. Then expect blessing.

Conditioning

When it comes to exercising self-control, the way you have conditioned your body is everything. *Ev-er-ry-thing.*

I don't know if there is a way to fully articulate a) how true this statement is and b) how important this statement is.

Here are a few quick points to know about conditioning:

Conditioning is a self-control key	Scientifically, it literally makes you and forms the matter of your makeup.
Conditioning is another word for train	Conditioning is like habit but instead of what you've trained yourself to do, it's what you've trained yourself to be.
Conditioning controls cravings	Conditioning is ultimately what controls what your body craves.
Conditioning can and often does lead to food addictions	Such as addiction to sugar, carbohydrates and even good things like arugula (too much of anything turns bad).

Conditioning your body is not rocket science. On the contrary, it is pretty elementary in principal and practice. Nevertheless powerful.

Whatever your body is fed it wants more of.

What you crave comes down to what you've conditioned your body to expect. I have personally experienced this in a powerful way.

Over about a year's time, I went from having pizza and ice-cream on Friday nights to fasting on Friday nights. Fasting! As in, abstaining from food.

This is the power of conditioning.

How did I do it?

It started out with me realizing (keyword) how much sugar I was feeding my body in such a short amount of time it would take me to eat. Between the sugar by body would turn into glucose from the pizza dough to the amount of straight sugar that was in a pint of ice-cream (yeah, I know, at least it wasn't a gallon, right? but still), it was an immediate reality check.

I realized that if I kept doing that I would eventually start to see and feel the ill effects of this. I had already noticed my stomach starting to pooch out a bit — which was honestly enough for the vanity in me.

Digression. This is a good time to remember the "revelation of the waistline" as I like to call it. Remember, it is our waistlines — where our vital organs are, and they are either thriving or merely surviving depending on your intake — not our weight are the barometer for how healthy we are.

So, besides the obvious of putting an end to having pizza and ice-cream on Friday nights, I started eating my normal healthy food that I consumed throughout the week on Friday's too and not having a cheat day[9].

So now the question becomes, if conditioning is really this simple why is it so hard to do? Here's the thing...

When you are conditioning or reconditioning your body, you must be willing to feel uncomfortable until you get over the hump.

You must be willing to get through the initial "pain" of not feeding your feel-good cravings. You have to be willing to get through the initial "pain" of not feeding your make me *feel* good cravings and be willing to suffer a little bit for the tremendous gain that self-control will bring to every aspect of your self and life.

Immersion

Go with me here. Really paint the picture. Imagine fish in a freshwater aquarium. Or, even better, a vast ocean. All colors, shapes and sizes of every sea creature named moving about gracefully and flourishing in every way.

They're immersed in their natural habitat. Water. Totally immersed. Totally immersed. Totally immersed. An intriguing phrase don't you think.

What does it mean to be totally immersed? What does it look like? And, more importantly, what would it look like for *you*?

The literal definition of *immerse* has an a, b and c definition:

a. *to dip or submerge in a liquid;*
b. *to involve oneself deeply in a particular activity or interest*
c. *to baptize (someone) by immersion in water.*

Like a fish, when you are immersed in something, mentally, there is nothing else around you except what you are immersed it. Mentally, you are completely submerged and surrounded.

For self-control, the idea of immersion is not so much physical (although this could be the case), as it is figurative.

Immersed in work or study. Immersed in rehearsal or practice. Immersed in problem-solving or critical thinking. Immersed in crafting or creating. Even, and unfortunately, immersed in unforgiveness. Offense. Fear. Worry. Anxiety. Grief. Stress. Depression. Addiction. And so on.

Some key qualities of this figurative, mental immersion are:
- Being in your element. Being in flow
- Extraordinary focus, which is its link to self-control. When you are immersed in something nothing else is in the picture nor can anything else creep into the picture because all of you is already taken. You are already fully submerged and fully surrounded by something.
- Being fully in. Just like a fish. Fully submerged and fully surrounded.

Now, to really bring this home, let's consider the inverse of immersion. What happens when a fish is out of water and no longer immersed in its element? It begins to suffocate and eventually dies. Fast.

Like fish, we too need to be immersed — fully submerged and fully surrounded — in things that cause us to flourish and thrive. Things that cause us to breathe and things that give us life.

With humanity's common purpose to become our highest and best selves, it is the responsibility of each of us to immerse our minds, our bodies, and our souls into that which will provide life. Life to ourselves and to others.

Let me repeat that. Our responsibility as humans, God's highest creation, is to immerse ourselves in things that provide life. Vitality. Health. Wealth. Wisdom. Light. Love. Understanding. Life application. etc. When we do – hear me – we thrive and not merely survive and tragically ally with death because of alternate unhealthy consumption of and immersion in raw feels.

When we rise to this responsibility, we will slowly but surely transform into something better than what we were born as.

You were made to create and to *always* be immersed in something creative and good for the greater good.

> *"My Father is always working and so am I."*
> *Jesus Christ*

The P Factor

Purity. This word has virtually become an ancient, and even offensive, word in our culture today. Even so, be aware that as you mature and increase in self-control, you will begin craving things that are pure. Things that are entirely good and good for you.

Impure things – what only looks, tastes and feel good – will become a complete turn-off as your cravings are reconditioned.

A nice little way to keep nudging yourself along in your journey of increasing self-control is to form the habit of asking yourself, *is it pure?* If it is pure, consume it. If it is not pure, can it.

Eenie Meenie Miney Mo

Choosing. Something you will have to do constantly when working to increase self-control. Literally up to a hundred-plus times a day.

I know this may sound a bit hyperbolic, but today with our busyness and culture of distraction and wasting time on things that don't have significant or lasting value (whatever is fun, easy and entertaining), it's not. Little things amount to big things over time.

When I first got into life coaching 20 years ago, the very first audio message I recorded was on choices. I remember carefully considering the topic of what I wanted to share for my very first message to my listeners and this was it. Here's the key takeaway:

Life <u>always</u> presents us with an opportunity to choose what is right.

Choosing is your will, your personal volition. It is also an act of control. To make it *self*-control would be to choose what is good and right over what merely feels good and is, ultimately, destructive.

Too, choosing is a God-given right and in the context of self-control it is a grace, or opportunity, to choose between good and evil. To choose what brings life or what brings death. To reach for purpose or to reach for fleeting and fruitless pleasure.

How amazing and gracious is it that we always get to choose the way we take in self-care, our actions, our dealing with others and in any situation or circumstance of life we find ourselves in.

Meditating on this advantage and opportunity often will increase your strength to choose well often (more often than not). With me?

Life Management

Someone once asked the question [a very loaded question I might add], *what is life?* Their answer was *life is time.*

I could not agree more. This life as we know it can honestly be summed up in this one little four-letter word. T i m e. Hence the well-known English phrase, "when your time is up," which refers to the physical death of our bodies.

While I am not able to do the slightest bit of justice — within the scope of my writing here — unpacking this vital subject, I will share one key thought, which is this: how we manage our time is how we manage our life. How we manage our time is how we manage our life..

Said another way, the way internationally known personal development guru Brian Tracy put it, time management is really life management.

"The essence of time management," he writes on page 191 of his book *No Excuses! The Power of Self-Discipline,* "is for you to discipline yourself to set clear priorities — and then stick to those priorities. You must consciously and deliberately select the most valuable and important thing that you could be doing at any given time, and then discipline yourself to work solely on that task."

This, by far, has been my biggest area of struggle with self-discipline. I spent *years* — a decade or more — spending and wasting time engaged in idle activities like (no pun intended) being on social media websites for hours at a time.

Brian goes on to write, "you can tell the value that something has to you by the amount of time you invest in it."

Having conquered time-waster demons and now being on the extreme other end as a productivity enthusiast, I can personally testify that if you can master time management — such as mastering getting out of bed or mastering dietary intake — you will experience radical change that will lead to breakthroughs in other areas of self-control you might be struggling in.

> *These particular areas of mastery are absolute game-changers.*

So remember that life is time. Life is time. Life is time.

Recall this often and, if you will, make an inner vow to yourself that you will not *spend* the time you have. Rather, you will *invest* the time you have in becoming your highest and best self then giving yourself (that is, your gifts, time, talents, treasure, skills) away to help others become their highest and best selves. And they, in turn, to do the same. And on and on and on.

Juice: An Essential Ingredient for Breakthrough

Before I begin, let me preface this section by boldly stating

What I am sharing here is <u>exactly</u> what you need to know in order to experience the breakthrough that you not only desire but desperately need.

If you really position yourself — that is, open your heart and mind — to receive the knowledge of what I am sharing and, in turn, continue on to incorporate some (if not all) of the self-control strategies found in Part B, you will experience your breakthrough and begin to flourish in becoming the person you see yourself as and doing the things you dream of doing. You will be on your way to fulfilling your maximum potential and ultimately your life purpose.

Do not downplay the power of words printed in a book to radically change your life. These are not merely words on a page. This is revelation knowledge that carries an anointing to uniquely speak to you where you are and lead you to experience breakthrough.

THE JUICE OF LIFE

Power. The juice of life as I affectionately refer to it as.

Often, we think of power in terms of authority but when it comes to personal development — which self-control falls under — power has another meaning that not many people are aware of.

Power is also the ability to take action and *personal* power is your ability to take action when it comes to bettering your *self* in some shape, form or fashion.

So let me repeat this because it's worth repeating now and later. Power is your ability to take action and personal power is your ability to take action when it comes to bettering your self in some way.

Increasing in self-control. Replacing bad habits with good ones. Ending self-sabotage. Letting go of limiting beliefs. Increasing your productivity. Forgetting fear and stepping out to fulfill your maximum potential. Overcoming a monumental obstacle. Doing something significant for the betterment of mankind.

> *Catch this: To take and keep taking consistent action <u>until</u> your goal is achieved is evidence of the personal power you possess.*

Hear me here. *If you have been struggling to understand why you have not been able to reach the place you earnestly desire to be, lack of personal power is one of the major reasons.*

In ministering to, counseling and coaching clients from all walks of life, I learn over and over that this is one of the primary reasons people are stuck. Stuck in the same place for *years*. Stuck in the same cycle of self-defeat and self-sabotaging behaviors and starting something but failing to follow-through and finish it.

Think about it. If personal power is the ability to take action and being stuck is not being able to move (zero action), the connection between the two can clearly be seen.

Realize this. You can have the right knowledge and all the will in the world, but if you don't have any personal power you will remain right where you are.

As I mentioned in the introduction, probably my favorite quote of all time is, "the great end of life is not knowledge but action." O how true this is.

> *At the end of your life, it is not going to be about what you knew. It's going to be about what you did.*

At this point, you might be wondering about the how, asking yourself, *how do I get to the place of personal power?*

For the answer to this question, consider the following comments from the famous Tony Robbins when speaking of his popular firewalk experience, where attendees of his seminar are given the opportunity to walk barefoot across a bed of hot coals:

> "The only difference between whether you can walk on fire or not is your ability to communicate to yourself in a way that causes you to take action, in spite of all your past fear programming about what should happen to you. The lesson is that people can do virtually anything as long as they muster the resources to believe they can and take the effective actions.
>
> The firewalk is an experience in personal power and a metaphor for possibilities, an opportunity for people to produce results they previously had thought impossible[10]. "

In other words, your juice level in life – your personal power – ultimately boils down to *the story you tell yourself*. Take this in for a moment before moving on. What is/are the story/stories you have been telling yourself? Are they based on truth?

Earn Your Eat™

As a triune being of spirit, soul and body, man cannot live on bread alone. We need spiritual food as much as we need physical food.

Yet, fruitlessly, many men and women go through life attending only to physical needs and never come to this vital realization; that physical food and any other physical matter will never wholly satisfy them. Again, this is because the physical body is only one part of man's triune being and physical matter is only one aspect of existence.

Now don't misunderstand me here. Our physical body certainly needs cared for and fed, but so do our soul and spirit. Truth be told, the superior latter — soul and spirit — need to be fed more.

Know this. Optimal health and well-being, mood, motivation and energy is achieved holistically from many other factors outside of eating food[11]. This (other factors) being established, what we eat is, nonetheless, a large part of achieving optimal health and well-being. Eating just isn't *all* of it as one could easily conclude based, by and large, on our food and drink appetites to the neglect of our spirits.

Contrary to popular belief, breakfast is not the most important meal. There is no such thing as "the most important meal."

Realize the truth that it is not so much about when we eat (although this does come into play), but about <u>what</u> we eat and <u>how much</u> we are eat that are the main things to consider and act from.

As I shared in Chapter 4, there is a difference between scientific hunger and appetite. It may be a good to go back and reread the Appetite section now or right after reading this section in order for these new thoughts — that I am sure seem a bit radical — to really resonate and settle in your current thinking about food and your relationship with food if it is not a healthy one.

Then, strategically and practically, your next step would be to form a habit of asking yourself if you are really scientifically hungry or if what you are feeling is just an emotionally triggered or conditioned craving harassing you to feed it? Or perhaps food digesting?

If it is just a harassing craving, it will pass after resisting it for a few minutes. Trust me. Further, the craving will pass quicker when you:

1) Change the story playing in your head from *I'm hungry* or *I'm starving* to *I am not really scientifically hungry* or *This is just a craving this is going to pass soon*.

2) Shift your focus to something meaningful or productive, remembering the transmutation method covered in Chapter 6.

Personally, I use my words to chase emotionally based and emotionally triggered cravings away.

I say out loud, *I am not hungry. You are just a pesky craving. You are not getting fed. Leave me alone. Go now. I am not feeding you. You are not getting fed.* I am saying these as I continue to work or, if I am not already working at the time, as I get to work on a current project, write or read until the craving subsides. I have never had to go more than a few minutes of doing this before the craving leaves.

These are the types of questions (in no particular order) you want to ask yourself before eating:

- Have I fed my unseen self, my spirit and soul yet?
- Have I drunk water yet?
- Have I had a bowel movement yet?
- Is it really time for me to eat?
- How long has it been since I last ate?
- Have I burned off what I last ate?
- Am I about to eat just out of habit and/or routine?
- Have I earned the right to eat big breakfast, lunch or dinner? Have I worked for this food? Have I expended a significant amount of energy to the point my body now needs refueled?

If you have not yet earned your eat, here are some simple strategies you can put into practice:

1. **Move your body.** Get up and burn some calories. Go out. Workout. Walk. Jog. Run. Ride. Whatever your activity preference is.
2. **Expend some mental energy.** Get to work! Tackle your most important task of the day before you eat. Identify your most important task (whatever would make today a win for you) and spend time doing this before you eat. Feel free to drink while you are doing it. Water to hydrate or whatever your choice. If you choose some caffeine, make sure you hydrate your body beforehand.
3. **Read.** Read something profitable. Something educational.
4. **Write.** Write something for your profession or journal whatever you feel inclined to write about.
5. **Plan.** Give thought to planning your day, week or month of most meaningful goals. Really give thought. Try not to rush through this exercise. Sit still beforehand. Listen to what God is saying to you. is saying to you. Look to the current lessons life is teaching you right now then start writing.

The point of all these is to, obviously, not just eat for the sake of eating but also to not add more food to your digestive system when what you last ate has not even come close to clearing out. Bodily activity helps move things along — which, speaking of moving — as I mentioned above, be mindful of your bowel movements and having enough of them before eating, eating, eating.

All these things will keep your body balanced and feeling great. These things will keep your bodily systems running and functioning and operating optimally and smoothly like a well-oiled machine.

A Harsh Reality

News flash: your body is not your friend. Your body is your enemy.

Just like the world we live in is enemy territory, our bodies are enemy territory too.

I know this might be a bit harsh to hear but I also know the sooner you realize *and* accept this truth, the better off you are going to be.

So right about now I can hear you thinking and questioning, huh? *What is she talking about my body is my enemy? How so?*

Well, for a huge starter, it naturally (keyword) betrays you.

Do you invite colds, the flu or other ailments to come upon you? Do you invite sickness and disease to come upon you? Do you invite the ungodly urges you have to come upon you? Do you invite death to come visit you? Can you control whether any one of these or other ills happen to your body or not?

Ultimately, no you cannot. No one can.

Granted, based on our intake (which is what we consume, which I get deep into later), to a degree we can control the extent and frequency to which we experience these things. But that's it.

My late play father Pierce's life ended tragically in his 50's with a high degree of pain and suffering from cancer, but it was ultimately due to his large intake of drugs and alcohol.

One unforgettable, physical effect these self-destructive substances (and consequential sickness) had on him was the swelling of his right thigh. It literally become the size of the widest part of a mini canon ball. It was massive and an incredible sight to see. Too, it was so hard and heavy that he could no longer walk without a cane. The seams of his pants had to be split in order to get them on.

But the pain he was in was by far the worst part. Severe, incessant pain that no prescription drug (including morphine) could make better. He would call me weeping, seeking to hear encouraging words to help him cope with the extraordinary amount of pain he was in from his leg. Encouraging words were the only thing that would "help" at this point.

I am sharing Pierce's story because it is a powerful example that we can all learn from.

Bad consumption can adversely affect our bodies in ways we could never imagine.

There are thousands upon thousands of fascinating (not in a good way) examples throughout history and today of how our bodies break down and become grossly marred by sickness and disease.

Let me open up and share another story with you. Honestly.

One morning at work, shortly after 11:00, the office aroma was that of food of various kind from people warming up their lunches in the microwave. The smell literally made me sick to my stomach. I began to think and pray silently in my heart, *to not be so "radical" and, more important, self-righteous and judgmental of others. After all, I eat. I eat microwaved lunch. I have a snack when hungry and even at times when I am not hungry.*

Still, my spirit-man was disgusted. The smell of processed, fast food literally made my stomach feel sick. I wanted to puke.

Why I am sharing this with you? Because in that somewhat surreal moment I had an important revelation. Which was this:

Our bodies are not only enemies but, just like an enemy, they are literally out to destroy us (all jokes aside).

And one of the biggest ways it seeks to do this is through the "food" we eat. And eat. And eat. And eat and eat even when we are not anywhere close to being scientifically hungry and we have not "earned" the right to eat again after having eaten anywhere between 1-4 hours earlier.

On the contrary, most of the time, we should refrain from eating when we get an urge to eat and rather drink something to push the existing food waste through our digestive systems and out of our bodies.

Note to self. There is something called *gluttony* and it can in fact lead to premature death.

When it comes to overconsumption of food, the consequences we suffer leading up to death is sickness and disease. Then death. *From food.* Something that is actually meant to keep us alive.

I sure do hope by now some of this is starting to sink in.

FOOD FOR THOUGHT

Death is the end of this physical life as we know it and, sadly, more often than not sickness and/or disease precedes it. Why? The elementary explanation is because these physical bodies of ours are not made to live forever.

Can I leave you with this short list of four fascinating (at least to me) food-for-thought about our bodies?

1. When we don't wash it, it starts stinking quick.
2. When it consumes a good-looking, good-smelling and good-tasting meal, it looks, smells and tastes anything but good when it passes through our digestive systems.
3. It is fragile and fickle. When it is too hot, it is uncomfortable and frustrated. When it is too cold it is also uncomfortable and frustrated. And if either of these are not

remedied rather quickly and escalate to extremes, you will find yourself in a life-threatening situation.
4. It is dumb. Our bodies are inanimate objects on their own (the spirit in you is giving life, or animating, your body; and when your spirit departs your body is dead).

You might be thinking at this point, *well, our bodies do us good as well.* You'd be right in this thought, with one caveat:

Our bodies do us good only when we respect the bad about them and act oppositely.

In other words, by way of self-control, we must recondition our bad-by-nature bodies to behave good in order to have a fighting chance of them being good back to us.

Otherwise, they subtly work in disguise through fleeting raw feel gratifications — such as food, sex and substance abuse — to bring premature death upon us.

"We have met the enemy and he is us." Pogo (Walt Kelly)

Her Hormonology

Ladies, this is a quick, cliff notes, crash course on your female hormone cycle and its significant effect on self-control (or lack thereof).

Fellas feel free to skip this section but don't feel like you have to because you will undoubtedly learn something valuable about your wife or significant other.

Hormonology. You might be wondering, *is this a real word or one I made up?* While not a word you hear every day, it is a real word.

The medical definition of hormonology is *a branch of science concerned with the study of hormones.*

I am willing to bet most women reading this is aware of the connection between their hormones and self-control. No news here. However, the real question is, how aware?

It is good to know that your hormones are affecting your mood, behavior and overall health but having deeper *how* knowledge will not only empower self-control but it will, even greater, cause you to think differently which will, in turn, inform your actions. Which, in turn, will alter your outcomes. Can you say *game-changer*?

My self-control game went through the roof when I got revelation of what I am sharing with you here. It played a major role in refining (keyword) self-control with my dietary intake and at-large.

Needless to say, but I will say it anyway, it is very important to realize this connection and, moreover, the effects your hormones have on you throughout (another keyword) your female cycle — which is constant throughout the month, which is contrary to the miseducation that your menstrual cycle is only when you are actually on your period. Make sure you catch this:

Your female cycle is nonstop.

Therefore, it is important to always be aware of where you are in your cycle. You can choose to keep track by week (like I do) or by day which is often necessary in light of exercising self-control as well as for advance planning of events, activities or special occasions (and many of you will add family planning to this list).

> **During Week One (Days 1-7)**: Estrogen begins to rise. As a result, your mood begins to boost. In general, you experience more energy, more optimism, more motivation, more patience, are more sociable, more daring, better at memorizing, communicating and learning new skills. You also build more muscle when exercising as well as feel more romantic and more interested in being close to your mate or future mate. As for food, your appetite is not as

strong so you will tend to eat less and more healthy options when you do eat.

During Week Two (Days 8-14): Estrogen and testosterone rise until they peak. Hormonal affects this week are the same as week 1 but better. You are your ideal self. A picture of confidence. Brave. And, you literally look more attractive because estrogen is prompting subtle shifts in soft tissue that make your facial features slightly more symmetrical. Be aware, though, depending on how your body deals with high levels of estrogen and testosterone, you could experience slight feelings of overwhelm and mild anxiety due to excessive arousal in your brain. As for food, your cravings are still healthy.

During Week Three (Days 15-22): Progesterone rises and estrogen and testosterone drop the first half of the week, then estrogen rises again. Your mood begins to go a bit downhill. Many women experience a "pre-PMS" during the first half of week 3. Due to dipping estrogen, you are likely to be irritable and more tired. However, the good news is this is short-lived. By the second half of the week, estrogen is rising again and putting a stop to your Pre-PMS Irritability. Fatigue, however, may stick around because progesterone is a sedating hormone. Not only does it bring about fatigue, it can also make you feel foggy, prone to crying more and mild constipation. As for food, your appetite is bigger and unhealthy food cravings begin to surface. You will be quick to reach for your favorite comfort foods and snacks. Interestingly, the bigger appetite is because your body is reacting to the possibility of you being pregnant (what may have happened during ovulation), so progesterone wants you to eat enough for two. Amazing fact, isn't it? So, during this time of your cycle, if you eat too little, you are going to be a very cranky girl. This is when eating more is actually healthy. Still, remember everything in moderation. Appearance-wise, you will be a bit bloated as a result of your body retaining water. Exercise-wise, you will burn up to 30% more fat when you exercise thanks to the combination of estrogen and progesterone making your body more efficient at using fat for fuel. Romance-wise, you may want to cuddle but not go any further than this. (Men: now you know why your wife or significant other is moody. Female hormones are much more active than male. We have a lot going on/shifting all the time!)

During Week Four (Days 22-28): The final week of your cycle, estrogen and progesterone plunge. The lower your estrogen goes, the more likely — this is especially true if you have poor eating habits — your good mood is to go with it. As a result, you'll be more sad, irritable, anxious and cynical/sarcastic. One very good thing to be grateful for this week is you begin to start feeling less tired and more energized because progesterone (the sedating hormone) is decreasing. Exercise-wise, you experience the same affects as week 3 in burning up to 30% more fat due to estrogen and progesterone awaking your body's fat-burners. Libido-wise, you may feel some energy due to nerve endings being stimulated as your body prepares for menstruation. As for food, carbs, carbs and more carbs. Bread, pasta and sweets. This is the time during the month where your cravings for fat and sugar go off the charts. This is because as estrogen is plunging, it causes levels of mood-moderating serotonin in the brain to drop and carbohydrates help to replenish it.

There you have it ladies. A quick and useful digested version of your female hormone cycle[12] and how they impact your mood and behavior. With this, you can now (on a daily basis) assess and act accordingly.

How would that look? For example, on a day where estrogen is really plunging, it might be a good idea for you to eat foods that produce estrogen. When progesterone is on the rise and thus sapping your energy, you may want to take an additional aerobics class that week so your body will produce more endorphins and make you feel more energized.

Best wishes my fellow female readers. May your lives and hormonal reactions forever be changed for the better from this day forward.

Ergonomically Speaking

Yes, surprisingly, Ergonomics matter when it comes to self-control. Let me share how.

If you do your homework you will find there is a compelling and fascinating body of recent scientific research around sitting versus standing and the health detriments and benefits of both.

In short, sitting too much for too long in one stretch of time is generally bad and standing is generally better. This is, by in large, because our business culture today (think desk jobs and sitting too long), but even more so because of our body's skeletal make-up.

Therefore, if your work requires you to sit at length, spending a little time to find your optimal stasis position when working is well worth the effort. When you do, it will increase your focus (which is a manifestation of self-control) and, in turn, your productivity (another manifestation of self-control and its cousin self-discipline).

I can personally testify to the truth of this. Being the enthusiastic, life-long learner and avid reader I am, I had read and held on to this knowledge for much too long before acting on it and, in doing so, reaping the tremendous benefits from it.

During long sessions of sitting (writing), I would remember to sit up as straight as possible and to not slouch the least bit. Posture on point. Shoulders completely square. And while this definitely helped, I was never "wowed" until one day I put a little more thought into it and went further by adjusting my chair to a different height and finding just the right level of closeness to/from the desk.

I was — and still am to this very day — both wowed and amazed at the incredible difference such a minor adjustment makes when I work. My sober-mindedness, motivation, enthusiasm, focus and, ultimately, productivity skyrocket.

Isn't this so good? If you agree, on your next opportunity, find your sweet spot while sitting and working. Self-control will soar.

Another Harsh Reality

This will be another hard pill to swallow for most. Humility.

When working to achieve any virtue, self-control included, we must be willing to admit we don't know as much as we like to think we know.

Let me repeat that: we must be willing to admit that we don't know as much as we think we know. That our ideas are just that — ours. And because of this, to some degree or another, we are bias to our own thoughts in spite of our best efforts to be objective.

Along with this willingness comes admission that in our own desire to gratify ourselves, we act foolishly. Which is to say, it is not that we *can't* exercise self-control, we just *don't want to*. We don't want to because we enjoy our unhealthy, uncontrolled behavior so much that we are frankly unwilling to contain our actions. Going back to The Great Exchange and The Big Questions talked about earlier, which can all be summed up in one simple, short but profound question: *am I willing?*

I am going to challenge you to think earnestly about this question now and beyond this moment. Ruminate on it and do so in the context of your answer to this question that is also a very challenging one: *who am I that I should get what I want when I want it?*

Again, humility. A hard pill to swallow but if you can stomach it, you will experience incredible breakthroughs in your life.

If you are a parent, this is something that you teach your children. That in life they cannot have what they want when they want it — no matter how much they kick, cry, and scream for something. Yet, in our adulthood we conveniently forget this parenthood principle and its apropos application to ourselves no less. We selfishly think we should have what we want when we want it. Wrong.

Could it be that pride, lust, sensuality, covetousness, gluttony and other ills of self just overcomes us and, because we constantly feed these unhealthy cravings, they gain control over us and eventually form bad habits and addictions that we end up actually defending because we want what we want when we want it and no one is going to tell us what to do or how to do it?

Ouch.

Hurts, Habits and Hang-ups

I know I don't have to tell you that a bad habit is called a bad habit for a reason.

Bad because it is something unhealthy (some unhealthy intake) that ultimately hurts your health and well-being.

If I were to lovingly say "stop hurting yourself," it would no doubt invoke an agreeable response in your mind and words. The issue, however, would be the fact that this is easier said than done. Bad habits and self-destructive cycles are indeed hard to break.

But it can be done. There is a proven process you can go through to get you out of self-sabotage and moving forward.

First and foremost is simply having the awareness of the possibility and process of self-sabotage. Second, having the knowledge and understanding of how to break its vicious cycle.

Here, I can only add a brief table summary and a practical application of this process I am referring to. As you might imagine, there is a lot more to this that is out of scope for the simplistic knowledge I am sharing here.

But this is a good start for getting self-sabotage into your consciousness to begin healing and freedom from it.

The four stages of the sabotage cycle are: *The Event*; *The Lie*; *The Reaction/Comfort*; *The Response*.

THE EVENT	The what. What happened to me that hurt me in some shape, form or fashion. Some events are moments and others are experiences over a long period of time.
THE LIE	The meaning I assign – which is usually the lie. The event is not what gets us stuck in an unhealthy cycle. It is the interpretation of the event that gets us stuck. This is the real culprit of self-sabotage.
THE REACTION	The way I avoid pain, anxiety, hurt or disappointment. What I do defensively to make sure those events, emotions, or the system I've developed to escape never happen again.
THE RESPONSE	The way others react to my defense. Others often react to the defense in ways that reproduce the event for me and perpetuate the cycle (known as Circular Causality, or Pseudo feedback).

Now, I am willing to bet the big question in your mind is *how?* How does one break this unhealthy cycle? The answer is actually really simple. Here it is:

Pluck the root — which is the lie — by replacing it with the truth.

Before a change in your behavior can take place, a change in your thinking must take place. A change in how you actually perceive reality. Tear down the lie by seeking truth and, moreover, *accepting truth regardless of how you feel and personal opinion.*

Here is an example of what a self-sabotaging scenario would look like. Study and digest it first then, when you feel comfortable enough, apply your issue(s) and replace lie(s) with truth.

    1. **The Event.** I was abandoned or rejected in some way.

2. **The Lie.** Nobody wants me. What happened to me was because I am not good enough. I was rejected because I am not loveable.
3. **The Reaction/Comfort.** I isolate myself and avoid authentically connecting with people. I want to be around people but fear rejection and abandonment, so I am standoffish.
4. **The Response.** People don't gravitate to me or invite me to things because of my standoffishness.

Patches

Dope feigns are known for needing to get their fix.

This, to me, is one of the most powerful pictures of brokenness because only something that is broken needs to be fixed.

But guess what?

Dope feigns are not the only ones who are constantly looking for a fix.

In a very real sense, to varying degrees, we all are. We all are constantly looking for and, subsequently, getting our fixes.

Food fixes. People fixes. Sexual fixes. Substance abuse (alcohol) fixes. Social Media fixes. Entertainment fixes and any other raw feel fix that gratifies our "feel-good" senses.

Why? Because we are broken. Every last one of us.

There is something about these bodies of ours that want to be gratified at all times (notice I did not use the word *satisfied*). The Bible calls this something indwelling sin. Philosophy calls it human depravity. Human reasoning calls it sensuality.

> *Whatever label put on it is really doesn't matter. What matters is knowing truth. Accepting truth and, in turn, responding well to truth and not rejecting it.*

Something you may have already learned through your own personal struggles is that the fixes our flesh craves are always raw feels and never amount to real fulfillment. As I've already shared, raw feels are temporary "feel-good" fixes, and what I call *patches*.

What is interesting to note about patches is the fact that they are designed to only be a *temporary* fix until something permanent is set in place. So, in other words, that temporary fix — that cigarette, that cake and ice cream, that last couple hours you spent scrolling your Facebook feed, etc — you seek is really a cover-up for something much more significant and satisfying that your soul is longing for.

Also significant, due to their design, patches are flimsy and come off easily. The patches of food, sex, substance abuse, etc. we use function in the same way: as flimsy, temporary fixes that wear off shortly after they are applied. Can you relate?

The key question, then, is how do we get past patching?

The simple "one-size-fits-all" answer I can give here is that increasing our levels of self-control to condition our bodies to crave less of the stuff that is no good for them tops the list.

The Process

Throughout the process of reaching your maximum capacity for self-control you are going to feel physically uncomfortable.

Very uncomfortable most of the time and, at times, extremely uncomfortable to the point of experiencing some mild physical pain (like I feel right now as a fast from food to finish this project).

This is because various aspects of your body are literally stretching beyond their natural condition. What is naturally comfortable very quickly starts to feel uncomfortable when altered. Like a fish out of water. It will feel (keyword) this serious.

> *The process of transformation through conditioning is painful but the end results are amazing.*

Take heart knowing you won't always feel (keyword) this way. Sooner or later you will reach the level of success you desire and relief will come by default because, through conditioning, you've altered your natural state into a new comfortable with control built into it.

One thing I want to point out while on the subject of comfort is the fact that your body feels so uncomfortable when it is not being gratified with something that is bad for it. This is further proof of the fact that our body is not an ally. Rather, it is an enemy as I covered above in the *A Harsh Reality* section.

Finally, when it comes to self-control, discomfort and often pain is unfortunately and fortunately what your experience will be characterized by. As I have found, and I am willing to bet you have to, that without experiencing something for yourself, you remain the same. Talk truly is cheap when it comes to exercising self-control.

> *You yourself must go through experiences in order to see change.*

Remember this nugget and one of our breakthrough principles (one I remind myself of often): pain strengthens while pleasure weakens. Pain strengthens while pleasure weakens.

Have you ever been through a tough time and came out so much better or stronger on the other side of that tough time? Of course.

And on the flipside, have you ever eaten too much ice cream or drank too much alcohol (both giving you sheer and utter pleasure at the time of indulgence) only later to have a terrible stomachache or headache from being hungover? Been there. Again, pain strengthens while pleasure weakens.

Your body feeling aches and pains and massively uncomfortable for not getting what it is screaming at you for is a good thing.

Really here me here. On the other side of it are the results you want. On the other side of the discomfort are the results you want. Unfortunately, there is something wonky about our bodies (that I teach in my THESE BODIES ™ training system) that require some discomfort in order for them to transform for the better.

The best way to position yourself to reach success in the process is to be ready for it. To anticipate it. To know in advance that the journey to becoming your highest and best self will not be easily traveled but, because you are ripe to see and experience real change for the better, you are decided and committed to going through the process. Decide now. Commit now. Be ready to feel uncomfortable now. Be long-suffering now. Be ready to deny yourself now. Are you with me?

Finally, the good news is, you can look forward to the fact that the process does get easier. The struggle is real during the initial "detox" period but after while your body does begin to adjust and the discomfort gets less and less. Never totally going away — which you would not want because you'll revert back to unhealthy, bad habits — but less for sure. You got this.

Notes

¹ Image source: *unknown*.

² Understand my protruding abdomen thoughts can be viewed as an extremist, radical perspective and, as such, will not entirely apply to everyone. Additionally, as I mentioned in the main text, there are of course perfectly valid exceptions for larger abdomen's like that of those with medical conditions; those that may have just had a baby; men and women that are naturally of larger frames/dimensions whose bulge is benign; those that are on a weight loss journey, and other exceptions.

My sincere and pure intention in sharing these thoughts is simply to *raise your level of consciousness* to the end that you should eat or not eat with these thoughts in mind. In sum, if your waistline girth is much wider than your hips, these thoughts may be for you.

³ Please know this is not an exercise to make you feel bad or an occasion to beat yourself up if you have a large waistline. Rather, please view this as a new beginning for yourself, as it is truly the start of your journey to the best and highest version of yourself.

⁴ Wattles, Wallace D. *The Science of Being Well.* Sterling Publishing Co., Inc. 2017. Page 158

⁵ Conger, Cristen "How Food Cravings Work" 18 August 2008. HowStuffWorks.com.
<https://science.howstuffworks.com/innovation/edible-innovations/food-cravings.htm>

⁶ Enjoying a drink or two will not poison your system but overdoing it to the point of intoxication and blacking-out will.

⁷ Howard, Jacqueline "For Stress, SuperFoods Are Better Than Comfort Food" 15 December 2016
CNN.com

[8] Learn more about Terri Andres' *Feed Responsibly*™ training system at harvesterinstitute.com

[9] If you're curious, my cheating would be a signature (err, sugary) drink from Starbucks (one of the ones that real coffee drinkers protest that that's not real coffee. And I concur. Hence my cheat treat), pizza and ice cream.

[10] Robbins, Tony. *Unlimited Power: The New Science of Personal Achievement.* Simon and Schuster Paperbacks. 1986. Page 15.

[11] What I mentioned above about feeding and nurturing our superior, unseen selves being the biggest factor.

[12] Shout out to Gabrielle Lichterman of MyHormonology.com for her fantastic, purpose-driven, content-rich website and apps on female hormonology. All the information Terri Andres shared in this section was taken from Gabrielle's website.

CHAPTER 5

Your No-Button-Zone: The Place Where Nothing Bothers You

Your no button zone is the place where very few things can bother you and cause you to come undone. It is consciously pressing in to exist in a surrendered state of mind and of self on a higher level of awareness to maximize the current moment with calmness and intentional thoughts, words and actions no matter what is happening to you or around you. (Translation: never flipping out)

Imagine a world where most people practiced this. The very thought of it stirs up positive emotion. If you took the time to imagine this, you know exactly the energizing feeling I am talking about.

My goal in this short chapter is to create more of this feeling for you to experience within your *self* and your life (every day routine).

The Art of Being

The art of being, aka the art of contentment, is an unexpected yet super effective strategy for self-control.

When you are content, you are at a state of peace. At a state of calm. At a state of rest. At a surrendered state of delightfully being and therefore you don't feel the need or have urge to reach for this or that to fill (err feel) up on.

Let that sink. Maybe even read it again.

When you have gained even the tiniest bit of mastery in the art of being, you are content with simply being. By default, your joy (internal) and happiness (external) increase as inner peace increases.

How many of you know that, in this glorified age of information and busyness we live in today, this would be quite an accomplishment?

When you start to master the art of being, you don't feel like you are missing out on something. For most human beings — less all the extraordinary soul's out there that don't easily succumb to the nth number of insatiable indulgences that overwhelm our senses — it's all about how he or she feels. So, to *not feel* like you are missing out on something is a big deal. Actually, it's an even bigger deal than that. It's monumental.

Another beautiful component of the art of being is gratitude. Expressing gratitude at any given moment, for any given thing, great or small, increases self-control because it is in these precious moments when you are most content.

Contained within contentment is control.

Did you catch that? Contained within contentment is self-control. When you are content and expressing gratitude, you don't want for anything – whether good or bad for you. You are grateful to simply be and are not trying to get into this or that to fill/feel up on. You are quiet and controlled in your thoughts and thus actions.

Are you seeing the power of this? How being still will keep you out of troubled waters? Because when you are still you are not doing anything. You are just being. Just. Being. Still.

Start to discipline yourself to be still when you are having urges to do this or that. Just. Be. Still. This will of course take practice — a consistent cycle of success and failure — and some will no doubt master it sooner rather than later, but the good news is being still is possible for everyone and it does not take any special gift, talent or skill. All it takes is awareness, intention, conditioning and practice.

Adult Time-Outs

Often a lack of self-control is the result of being in a state of stress or frustration.

Some fear, upset, worry, anxiety, anger, relationship woe, work incident, etc. has you bent out of shape and seeking some sort of pleasurable relief as an escape from the stress and frustration you are experiencing.

Instead of going with your first gut reaction, take a time-out.

Sometimes all you need to do is close your eyes and take a few deep breaths to disarm anxiousness.

If this isn't enough, fresh air might be what's needed. Get up, get out and go for a walk, run or drive.

If these don't work, seek solitude to get yourself into a state of calm. Do nothing outside of breathing deep and meditating for at least 10 minutes.

Last, but most importantly, the key thought I want you to take away here is that you will need to *make a decision* to time-out and get yourself in a better state instead of just going with what will most definitely come natural to you – which is typically bad and regretful.

CHAPTER 6

Your Self-In-Action: Stepping Up Your "A" Game

Now that you are starting to experience breakthroughs and increase in self-control, it is apropos to start addressing (provide knowledge and strategy) for some common areas of human deficiency as it relates to self-control and beyond – energy, creativity, potential, productivity and purpose.

Individuals who are particularly interested in discovering their purpose or getting to the next level in it will get a great deal of value out of this chapter as well as Chapter 8, *Your Kit and Caboodle to Start Crushin' It*.

Confidence

Confidence, or believing in yourself and your ability to do something, is another important element of self-control. As I touched upon right out the gate in the Introduction, you must *believe* you have what it takes within you to exercise self-control at any time you choose.

Can I be honest with you? Confidence is something I never thought I would ever lack. But when I started my first business (a life coaching practice), I failed mostly because I could not get my marketing right. I remember working so hard trying to get this particular piece to come together — knowing the success of the business was riding on it.

I cannot tell you the number of times I created a new document outlining my brand, my voice, and target audience.

Well, long story short, 4 years later, successful and confident in a new business, my brand, my voice and target audience are exactly the same as I'd outlined them the first time around.

The sole problem was I did not believe in myself. I did not believe I could get people to pay attention to — and pay — a coach to help them overcome their struggles with self. I did not believe my personality was dynamic enough to draw people to me and I did not believe I could market myself in such a way.

But the worst part was I didn't even know it. I didn't know I was deficient in this area.

I can see it today because of hindsight but more so because I have confidence now. I know how it feels. I know what it looks like. And, most exciting, I know what it makes me capable of. Its energy is unmatched.

Confidence is something that can be learned.

Just ask world-renowned Stanford University psychologist Carol S. Dweck.

In her book, *Mindset: The New Psychology of Success,* writes this about confidence after receiving a letter from a woman who had always struggled with confidence but after reading about one of Dweck's main ideas — having a growth mindset whereby one's focus is on learning and improving instead of solely on inherent ability:

> "A remarkable thing I've learned from my research is that in the growth mindset, you don't always need confidence. What I mean is that even when you think you're not good at something, you can still plunge into it wholeheartedly and stick to it. Actually, sometimes you plunge into something because you're not good at it. This is a wonderful feature of the growth mindset. You don't have to think you're already great at something to want to do it and to enjoy doing it.[1]

The reason I shared this with you is, like me not that long ago, you may not know that you lack confidence.

You may not know that the reason you feel like self-control is out of your reach only because you don't believe in yourself. That you can take control of whatever has control of you.

O but I am so glad you are reading these words. Remember, I was on the right track but lack of confidence caused me not to see this truth.

You, dear reader, I believe are on the right track but lack of confidence may be causing you not to see it.

So, take a baby step and start believing by affirming these facts: you are already confident or you can learn to be confidence when you focus on learning and improving in the area you are deficient in.

A Little Secret of Self-Control

There is a secret to self-control: focusing more energy on doing the right thing instead of the wrong thing. Focus more on doing what is right versus trying not to do what is wrong.

What happens when we are trying to improve some aspect of our self or our life, in the process of getting from where we are to where we want to be, we tend to focus on what we are not yet and we maximize our mess-up's to the point where we eventually get discouraged and throw in the towel. Thinking we will never reach success.

Well here is what I have learned to be a secret weapon: focusing my energy on what I can for sure do right. Whether that is exercising some form of self-control - like finishing a project for example.

The concept I am conveying is the same as the saying, "the quickest way to get over a lost love is to find a new one." Basically, not focusing on your broken heart, rather focusing on a new love.

It's all about where you choose to direct, or focus, your energy and this certainly applies to self-control.

Now, then, having said all that, understanding that focus is easier said than done, it will help you to understand how focus works so yours can increase.

What we focus on comes from what we've conditioned ourselves to focus on. Let me repeat that. What we focus on comes from what we've conditioned ourselves to focus on. Which is rooted in the following two things:

1. What we think on most (what we meditate on)
2. Our dominant emotional states

Our mindset and our emotional state — both of which determines our will to act a certain way.

The good news is we can train ourselves to focus on good things.

In Psychology, this practice is called Priming, which is where words, ideas, and sensory experiences color our perceptions of the world and affect our emotions, motivations and actions.

Therefore, be both aware and intentional about your choice of words, the ideas you allow into your head and your sensory input — what you take in through any of your five senses. You are being conditioned by all of it.

Switching Gears

Catch this. The urges you get are just energy and instead of using that energy to do something you don't want to do, you can use that energy to do something you do want to do.

Read that again.

Have you ever wondered why you get the urge to speed up and drive fast, border line reckless, at times? When you're on the interstate and before you even realize it you are speeding up or speeding around someone when you are not even in a rush?

The self-control strategy to not do this is to *reverse,* hence "switching gears."

When you get the urge to speed up, use this urge as a trigger to do the opposite. Instead of speeding up, reverse and slow down.

This is such an effective strategy for becoming more controlled because in a hair of a moment like that it is such a working of the will to act against your first urge.

I practice this all the time and, now, it is not so strong of a gut "umph" reaction. And it takes less effort every time, which further speaks to just how simple yet great of a self-control strategy it is.

The key to switching gears is <u>being aware</u> of your ability to do this.

This is a concept called Transmutation, an interesting notion that is widely studied and written about as well as being a popular strategy commonly used in personal development.

Transmutation is simply changing states.

The English Oxford dictionary defines it as *the action of changing or the state of being changed to another form.*

This process became popularized in the book *Think and Grow Rich,* which is where I first learned of it as it relates to self-help.

Transmutation ties right into what we just talked about in the previous section *A Little Secret to Self-Control* section; which is to focus — put more energy into — doing what is right than on trying not to do something you really don't want to do.

What a powerful strategy to add to your self-control arsenal of strategies. Game.

Self-Control Chunking

Developing and increasing your level of self-control is kind of like chunking in goal setting.

Chunking is *the grouping together of information into ideally sized pieces, so they can be used effectively to produce the outcome you want without stress or shutdown.*

Because we are so overwhelmed by our busyness and other sensory input that today's world of technology bombards us with, it's easier than ever for us to lack focus and/or be confused about what our focus should be. This is because, as research shows, humans are only able to focus on a limited number of things at once. Our brains are not designed for nor good at network switching.

Chunking helps remedy this because it effectively brings our desires (what we want to do) and to-do's (what we must do) into focus. Focus is a big key in self-control. Think of when you need to be super focused to finish something under a tight deadline. You shut down all distractions beforehand and when something unimportant tries to interrupt your focus, you shut it down right away. This is an essence of self-control.

Here is a 1-2-3 step on how chunking can be applied to increase self-control:
1. **Capture.** Get everything out of your head and make a list of your desires and to-do's.
2. **Chunk.** Organize your list by chunking, or categorizing, each entry in one of these 5 major areas of life: self/spirituality/religion; health and well-being; relationships; finances; and education/career.
3. **Notice.** Summarize what the ultimate outcome is for each of your chunks.

Once you know what your desired ultimate outcomes are, you will be able to *focus* on achieving your desired outcomes. Now, since you have a clear aim, your motivation will increase and you will come up with a clear plan of action to execute.

Self-control is not something that is handed to you or something you can buy.

It must be developed over time chunk by chunk through intentional focus and one "small" controlled decision after another. Then another. Then another. And so on. (Note that I put the word *small* in quotes because no controlled action you take is small and should never be minimized. Every act of self-control is a big deal).

Today, there are so many things vying for your attention in life — some legitimate responsibilities and other stuff insignificant, unimportant and lacking lasting value. If you don't make a conscious effort to decide what is important to you (your values) and therefore what you are going to focus your energy on, you will live in reaction to the demands of the moment. *Live in reaction* is an opposite of self-control.

It has been rightfully said that focus is the ultimate power that can change the way we think, the way we feel and what we do in any moment.

When we shift our focus to important things that matter and have lasting value, we change our self and our life.

Avoiding The Ugly P Word

Perfectionism.

There are two aspects of this I want to bring forth. One is, of course, as it relates to self-control. The other is as it relates to progress — which I will address first.

It is not possible (I've tried) for me to articulate how evil of an obstacle this can be. The literal definition for this English noun is *refusal to accept any standard short of perfection.*

From giving earnest thought to this for years, my conclusion is this: that the issue is not that perfection cannot be achieved. The issue is as flawed, performance-based humans with flawed thinking, individuals create their own ideas of what perfection is and looks like —something unattainable — instead of going on about the business of creating something and it being perfection. (Read that again. It's breakthrough knowledge.)

> *I call this perverted perfectionism. Because, ultimately, it's a perversion of truth.*

Its definition would be a fallen and false view of perfectionism that hinders significant progress. An evil perversion of a pure grade of perfectionism that is good and virtuous and attainable.

Pure perfection is possible. It is attainable by its definition: a) *the condition, state or quality of being free OR AS FREE AS POSSIBLE from all flaws or defects; b) a person or thing perceived as the embodiment of perfection; or c) the action or process of improving something until it is faultless OR AS FAULTLESS AS POSSIBLE.*

Perverted perfectionism was the root of a few things for me. It caused enormous lack of belief and confidence, not just in myself, but in my purpose. It caused me to believe that writing and becoming a professionally published author was too difficult and too hard of a task for me, hence unattainable. It also caused me to believe whatever I did do was not good enough and would never be good enough.

As if these were not bad enough, the worse part was the fact that I did not even know. I did not know this evil form of perfectionism is what was keeping me stuck. When, through self-help reading, I started to have some sense that my stuckedness was related to perfectionism, it was still years before I experienced breakthrough and true freedom.

The missing piece was the "perverted" part of this thing. That it was my own perverted ideas of perfection (that is, in reality, good and possible) that was holding me back.

> *Fortunately, and unfortunately, it was all in my head.*

So, here is what I want you to do. Identify which of these 3 categories you might fall in if perverted perfectionism is hindering your progress:
1. Those who never start
2. Those who start strong but don't finish
3. Those who start and finish but its "not good enough"

Awareness is paramount and the first step to any change. Once you locate yourself, with the breakthrough knowledge I have shared here coupled with your continued efforts in your personal development/transformation, you will find yourself unstuck and moving forward in no time.

Switching gears to perfectionism as it relates to self-control, yes, your striving is self-control, but it is imperative that you understand you are not striving to *be perfect* — which is completely different from the perfection unpacked above in the context of progress.

There are few things in this life more fruitless than trying to be perfect. Because, unlike perfection which is attainable in doing and creating (key phrase), it is not attainable in being.

No human being has ever or will ever reach perfection. It is not within human capacity. Only God is perfect. Every other being is opposite of this. "For all have sinned and fallen short of the glory of God." (Romans 5:3)

Move From Procrastination to Productivity

In my journey to operating in my purpose full-time, I have learned 5 major keys that will move anyone from procrastinator to bona fide producer who consistently creates.

#1. BASELINE

Remember at the beginning of Chapter 2 we talked about *The Baseline*? Well, here we go again. (If you don't remember, go back and refresh your memory before reading this so it will make greater sense and have greater impact).

Productivity ultimately comes down to a heart issue. It was not until I had this revelation that I started to experience breakthrough in the issue of procrastination being a part of what defined my character. It is painful just to even type these words!

> *Whatever has the biggest place in your heart is what you give attention to and, moreover, what you act on.*

Further, when your heart is set on something, very little (if anything) will stand in your way in seeking to satisfy your heart's desire. Like:

- When you are in love with him or her, you do any and everything in your power to be with your beloved.
- When you want that new handbag, ladies, or that pair of shoes that you just can't live without.
- When the big playoff game is airing, guys, and absolutely nothing will stand in the way of you watching it alone or with your homies.
- When, Mom, you are helping your daughter prepare for her wedding day.
- When, Dad, you are preparing to take your son on his first fishing trip.
- When, Grands, you get to spend quality time with your grandchildren.
- When birthdays, christenings, wedding anniversaries, etc come around.

Whatever it is, understand that what is biggest in your heart has your attention and, in turn, your actions and, in turn, your outcomes.

So while you may be well aware of your purpose and things you should be doing or have a desire to do, until they occupy a big enough space in your heart you will put them off. And somewhat automatically, I might add, because the other things that *do* occupy a big enough space are what have your attention and actions. Make sense?

#2. WHAT YOU VALUE

What you value, or what is most important to you. Know this, that your actions give you clues on what you value. For example, do you choose to eat over getting your most important task done? If so, this may be a clue that you value food *more*, which is the keyword here. Eating does not necessarily mean you don't value getting your task done. However, if you are not truly, scientifically hungry and ate just an hour or two earlier, this can be a strong indication that you value food *more than* getting important tasks done.

INTERMISSION

Let's pause from the 5 keys to unpack the element of self-control at play with procrastination. In a common situation such as this — eating over working — know this: whatever offers immediate gratification will undoubtedly have the strongest pull on your actions. But here is how you deal with that. You coach yourself and take time out to ask yourself a powerful question. When you ask the right questions you get the right answers. So, ask yourself right now, what do I value most? Eating this or getting the result that completing this task will produce in my life? And what we value is determined by — you guessed it — what is in our heart.

#3. THE STORY YOU TELL YOURSELF

The story you tell yourself in your moment of decision. This is the game-changer. The practical strategy and necessity. Being a procrastinator or producer boils down to the choices you make and what will enable you to make the best choice for you in achieving your goals is this right here: the story you tell yourself when it is time for you to make a choice in that oh so precious moment of decision that we talked about earlier. One thing my father has always told me is, making decisions is what make you an adult. In essence, what he is saying is it is *on you* as a mature adult to make a decision versus looking outside of yourself for someone else to make the decision for you. Hashtag: #PersonalResponsibility.

#4. ZEAL

Or enthusiasm. This is an amazing energy that propels you forward with little to no effort from you. I have always been intrigued by zeal and have studied it in-depth over the years. Rather naturally (before my studies), it became my go-to emotion when I needed to put my game face on when I find myself in a less-than-desirable emotional state like being tired from not getting enough sleep or if I am feeling nervous speaking publicly. Instead of telling myself over and over how tired or nervous I am, I tell myself how excited I am for an instant pick-me-up every time. Except, enthusiasm being what it is, it is more like an instant take-me-way-up. Enthusiasm, if you learn how to use it to your advantage, elevates your being, your energy, your productivity, your well-being ultimately the quality of life.

#5. GRIT

I define grit as simply having enough substance in you to press through obstacles. This is an attribute that we need today with time not being on our side and the never-ending temptations and seductions to take the fun, easy and entertaining route that not only keeps you stuck where you are in a fruitless, self-defeating pattern (aka, going in circles).

When you have grit you not only press through, but you press through with a sense of urgency and not lazily.

Form a habit of asking yourself these two worth-their-weight-in-gold, goal-achieving questions:
1. What is the most valuable use of my time right now?
2. What is the highest value task I can do right now?

#QOTD: Are You A Creator or Consumer?

Let what I have shared in the last two sections sink in and after soaking awhile, the question to ask yourself is simple but powerful. It is this: will I be a creator or will I be a consumer?

Will I use the gift of time I am given to create, to give and to add value to others? Or will I use the gift of time I am given to consume — to take and add only to myself? Will I be a wise investor or a wasteful spender of this precious gift of time I am given?

I mentioned this earlier in Chapter 4, but it is worth mentioning again here. Someone once asked the question, *what is life?* The answer given was, life is time. Enough said.

Partnering With Someone

There are three aspects I want to share about partnering with someone on your journey to increasing self-control: 1) when it is a very good thing; 2) when it is not; and 3) accountability.

#1. WHEN IT IS A VERY GOOD THING

It is difficult to articulate how vital it is to be united with someone else in some capacity. What I mean by this is connected to another person or group and operating together for a common cause.

This strengthens self-control in that you must get along with someone else. You must work with them and often this requires consistent self-sacrifice. Patience. Giving. Humility. Compromise. Forgiveness. Love, etc. You learn all these virtues – that require self-control – when you are united to others with the ultimate goal becoming one and operating as one. This takes a ton of control.

#2. WHEN IT IS NOT

Using another person for motivation is good but you have to know that it is not the "end all be all" to you developing self-control.

> *The actions of another person should never be used as a fix for our personal struggles.*

The reason is simple. Because people change. And the reality is people will let you down whether intentionally or unintentionally.

Understand that it is easy to look at other people as a source of motivation. Actually, it's natural. Why is this?

I am convinced a big reason is because man was made for worship. Worship in its basic, reduced form is simply looking outside of self to something else. Receiving something from what you're looking to and then acting upon what you've received (gleaned might be a better term).

The challenge for each of us *individually* is to make the decision and commitment to self-control not because of another person but because it is right for you and because it is good and right for all of us.

I can hear you saying, *easier said than done*. True but keep reading. I am confident that by the end of this book you will be adequately equipped to exercise self-control.

#3. ACCOUNTABILITY

If you are serious about self-control, you will make sure you have accountability in your life. Some person or group of people to whom you answer to for the state of your being (character) and in your behavior (actions). Because, remember, self is naturally uncontrolled hence the need for self-control and law (civil, criminal and moral) for that matter. Just as public laws of the land keep our wild human nature in check for others, your personal accountability team will serve as the law of your life to keep you in check for yourself.

The Importance of Not Overdoing It

Our egos are good at getting us to bite off more than we can chew, which is why it is so important to know where *you* are (versus where someone else is) so you can set your self-control goals accordingly.

This is especially the case when you are partnering with someone to keep you motivated and accountable on your journey to increased self-control.

Simply put, know your current capacity.

Know what you can and cannot do today and stay within these boundaries. Don't measure your progress by what you see happening or not happening in someone you admire from a distance or someone close to you.

I cannot stress how important it is for you to be in tune your own body in terms of your physical and mental health and well-being.

Using wisdom is the key.

Let me share a story from my life on how I overdid it.

It was during my first stint as an entrepreneur. I was trying hard to define my voice in order to get my marketing and sales strategies together and off the ground. After too long, ideas still were not gelling into something solid. As a side effect, I was also struggling with my content creation. To get over this hump, I felt like I needed to fast. So I did. I fasted for 31 days.

The fast included praying for an hour 3 times a day (at sunup, noon and sundown); a diet similar to the Daniel Fast (but stricter) and abstaining from all forms of fun, news, information, entertainment, moves, and of course social media.

As spiritually strong and in tune I was, this fast nearly broke me. Praying for an hour 3 times a day for 31 days was beyond challenging. It begot amazing results in terms of closeness to God but, nonetheless, extremely challenging.

Overall, the good result of this fast was I did experience several immediate breakthroughs I needed.

However, the bad was that not too long after this fast, my daily routine severely lacked the discipline it needed as an entrepreneur, ultimately, because I was "over" being so strict on myself after 31 brutal days of being that way.

Here's the worst part. Believe it or not, this turned out to be a *major life setback*. It adversely affected the trajectory of my life due to how far it knocked me off track and how long it took me to get back on track on the track I needed to be on – close to two years!

Here are the key takeaways on the various aspects of the importance of not overdoing it:

- Too much of anything — even healthy, profitable things — is bad. Needless to say, it is important to set reasonable goals for where you are. Have the right expectations.
- Similar to the above point, self-control and self-discipline are required to abstain from unhealthy behaviors, but they are also equally important to abstain from doing too much of the right thing. As the saying goes, everything in mod-

eration. There is a golden ribbon of truth in this. I found this out the hard way.
- We also need self-control when it is time to stop working and go home and be with your family. Working in and of itself is a good thing, however not when it threatens your relationships.
- When it is time stop helping that relative or friend that won't do for themselves and you have gone far beyond the point of helping but rather are only enabling and feeding self-defeating behavior in him or her.

Are you with me on these? I sure do hope so.

Notes

[1] Dweck, Carol S. Ph.D., *Mindset: The New Psychology of Success*. 2008 Ballantine Books Trade Paperback Edition, New York; pp 52-53

CHAPTER 7

Your Opposites of Good: Land Mines To Look Out For

The term *land mine* is one you don't hear much – if ever – as a civilian citizen of a nation. But it is a term that is very much a regular part of the vocabulary of war and military jargon.

So what is it exactly and, moreover, how does it relate to your self-control (or lack thereof)?

Its first known use was back in 1890 as a description for *a mine usually placed just below the surface of the ground and designed to be exploded usually by the weight of vehicles or troops passing over it.* Merriam-Webster's dictionary also adds that *land mine* is a term that is often used figuratively. For example, "*a political land mine.*"

There is no wonder for me why land mines are often used figuratively. Because there is never a shortage of things that are not in plain sight or obvious but are designed to destroy you when you get close enough or by outright going there. Whether it is unseen resistance or some evil catch that is purposely hidden, land mines exist to trap and ultimately kill.

Pause for reflection. *What figurative land mines have you gotten too close for comfort or stepped on? What's the way out? How do you get loose? Can you do it yourself or do you need to use one of your lifeline's to "call a friend" for help?*

The T Factor

Self-control requires resisting temptation that may not look like temptation on the surface – sounds like a land mine to me.

> *When you consciously start exercising self-control, immediately, you are going to experience opposition.*

Think about something you recently or at some point in the past resolved to do or not do. As soon as you made the resolution, it got even harder to do or not do.

In one sense – conceding there are several perspectives– this opposition can be viewed as temptation.

Here are a few examples of what I mean:
- *When you resolve to stop eating sweets, someone in your office brings in donuts – and not just any donuts, but "red light" donuts – the very next morning.*
- *When you resolve to stop watching triple X-rated programming, it coincidentally shows up on your TV or mobile device.*
- *When you resolve to stop drinking, your best friend asks you to join him or her for drinks to celebrate something.*

- *When you vow to work on that important project later when you get home, you're reminded that the season finale of your favorite TV show is airing.*

Again, the moment you make a conscious decision to exercise self-control, opposition, or temptation, starts to form against you.

Unfortunately, this is just the way it works in the wonky world we live in. So the question is, how do you overcome it?

For one – and this is huge for me – you must shift your mindset.

View the opposition as an <u>opportunity</u> for victory.

Second, be aware. Amplify your awareness. Now that you know what to expect when you start seriously exercising self-control, be on the lookout, always having top of mind that a) you are more than likely facing a temptation; b) the fact that you have a choice to make (resist or give-in); and c) the fact that you have the *opportunity* to make the right choice for yourself.

This opportunity is what I refer to as that *oh- so-precious moment of decision*. And, make no mistake, it is a fleeting moment. The second or two that life *always* presents you with to make a decision. To make a choice. To go right or left. To make the best decision or the bad decision.

You get to choose. Let me repeat that. You. Get. To. Choose. Your turn. Say it out loud right now, *I. Get. To. Choose.*

This is good news!

Now you might be asking at this point, *how do I choose the best decision in my moment of decision?* The answer is, you pause. Pause to tell yourself the truth, affirm your true identify and ask yourself powerful questions.

Here are a few examples of how that inner dialogue might go:
- *What is true in the situation right now?*
- *What do I really want? What am I really longing for?*
- *Right now, I have the power to choose the best thing for me in this moment.*
- *I have self-control and lots of it.*
- *I am an overcomer.*
- *I am a winner.*
- *I am victorious.*
- *What is the best action I can take for myself right now in this moment?*
- *How do I really want to feel right now? Not the raw feel but the real fill?*

When you know you are being tempted, this immediately *empowers* you because you can now *choose* what you will do versus just going with your natural instinct as a result of the bad habits and unhealthy cravings you are in the process of getting rid of.

Temporary Delays and Setbacks

These amount to the land mines of discouragement that leads to depression that leads to doubt in your ability to change.

So you remain the same or worse in self-sabotaging behavior until you eventually explode.

Just to be clear, by *delay* I mean being side-tracked momentarily but bouncing back without being completely set back. By *setback* I mean really being knocked back a square or two or back to the beginning.

In either case, know and accept beforehand that, inevitably, one or both will happen during the course (keyword phrase) of you are strengthening your self-control.

As I have already touched upon several times in earlier sections, delays and setbacks are an inherent part of this process. Just like failure is an inherent part of success.

Both are ultimately working for you and not against you despite what is currently happening to you or around you.

Know and accept the truth that delays or setbacks do not disqualify you and are not signs for you to give up.

> *You are never down and out unless you decide to be.*

Should you experience a temporary delay or setback, use these 5 simple steps to get back on track:

1. **Realize.** Know that this is just a mere delay or setback and an inherent part of success.
2. **Accept.** Come to terms quick with what is happening to you and/or around you – especially if it is something out of your control. No getting stuck from something outside your control allowed.
3. **Believe.** Trust that self-control is in you and is being developed more and more. Trust in your ability to bounce back from this. Build yourself up by using affirmations.
4. **Expect.** Look for your strength to rise. Trust me, it will show up as you continually do.
5. **Keep moving forward.** Continue onward in the renewed strength that comes from knowing with each delay or setback you are getting stronger and closer to your goal.

You got this.

CHAPTER **8**

Your Kit and Caboodle to Start Crushin' It: Next Level Living

Title translation: the purpose and productivity chapter.
Everyone reading this has a significant purpose and is called to create (or, produce a lot, which is effectively what productivity means) around that purpose in a unique way.

I know many of you reading this have heard this or some flavor of it too many times to count and are therefore nonchalant about it at this point because you still have not discovered what your purpose is. I hope to change that with what I am about to share – an abundance of useful and practical knowledge on your passion, purpose, productivity, making these happen and overcoming obstacles. All wrapped in the context of self-control.

As a person purposed with helping others find theirs, a productivity enthusiast, a goal-setter and goal-getter, and procrastination overcomer, I had a lot of fun researching and writing this chapter. I hope you get a lot out of it – and you will if you go beyond reading to acting on this transformational knowledge.

Passion

A lot can be said about passion and it is defined in several ways. How this really comes into play with self-control is, when you are denying yourself from instant gratification and the guilty pleasures of life, you must have something more important than these things as your *why*.

This something more is your passion.

Your purpose (which I will dive into next) in a simple few words is what you are here to do and finish. Your passion is the fuel that enables and empowers you to execute your purpose – particularly when facing opposition. Passion is what makes you keep going.

Something subtle that sucks your passion is idly waiting. Operating in neutral *wait* mode to make any significant moves toward your purpose because you are waiting for this, that or the other. Idly waiting for what you want.

> *When you are idly waiting you are not working. You are not creating.*

To be clear, what I mean by idly waiting is when you are *only* waiting (and doing nothing else) for what you want to happen within yourself or some aspect of your life.

Idly waiting consumes your energy and sucks life from you. Because the fact is, you don't have what you want yet you are *longing* for it. You become drained and lifeless because usually the wait is long. Years. Years of *eager* anticipation because this is something you really, really want so every part of you is all-in, 100% invested in your mind, will and emotions. Completely consumed by something that has not happened and is not happening. Something that is not a reality.

> *Idly waiting is an enemy of self-control, which productivity stems from.*

Think of idly waiting and passion as opposite nouns. Waiting is being still. Passion moves you.

On the other hand, however, there is such a thing as waiting well. Which is simply working and creating while you wait. You are waiting for what you want while at the same time (key phrase) moving forward in your life purpose. In this way of waiting, self-control is not an issue.

If idly waiting describes you, don't beat yourself up. Decide today to partner with your purpose and wait well for what you want. You'll be so happy you did and, as you do, your self-control will increase thus the quantity (productivity) and quality of your life will improve.

Your Purpose Box

When God has a purpose and He creates a person to fulfill it. Purpose comes first, then the person.

> *For every person born, a "purpose box" is also born.*

One day as I was pondering thoughts about purpose, God gave me a vision of purpose as a box — a box full of the tools that enable a person to fulfill the unique purpose for which they were created and consist as long as they do.

Note the following points about a purpose box:

- **It squashes comparisons.** Since purpose is unique to the person, the contents of our purpose boxes are different. So, feel free to squash all the comparisons you've ever made or are currently making between yourself and someone else. To continue them after getting revelation of what I am sharing here would be, with all due respect, foolish.
- **It squashes fear.** Something else to know and truly love about your purpose box is the fact that it is yours. Your name is on it. It is assigned to you. You are the only one that can access what is in your box. The unique things only in your box belong to you and no one else can lay claim to them. But know this — and this is something big — that with your box belonging only to you comes *a great responsibility to use the tools that have only been given to you.* Let me repeat that. You have the great responsibility to use and manage the tools (gifts, talents and time) that have been given only to you. Imagine coming to the end of your days on earth and you have not used what was given only to you? Unthinkable. I would not want to be in that position. So, with all this, how does your purpose box relate to self-control? The answer takes us to the final point.
- **It squashes unhealthy habits and behavior.** Here's the thing: *you have to partner with your purpose and it takes self-control to do this.* You must make a decision to partner with your purpose. To decide that no matter what, you are going to do the necessary work on your self and the affairs of your life to position yourself to operate in and ultimately fulfill your purpose.

> *Your purpose box is yours. It has your name branded on it. It is assigned to you and no one else can access it but you.*

This means you and you alone must take action and do something with what has been given to *you*.

Practically, this is what it will look like to partner with your purpose and use the tools within to fulfill your purpose — your supreme reason for being.

Last but not least, know that it takes self-control to partner with your purpose in that you will need to say *no* to spending (wasting) time doing what is fun, easy and entertaining.

You will have to say *no* to momentary pleasures and sacrifice these moments to live out the unique way you are called to serve others and make the world a better place while at the same time building a better tomorrow for yourself and your loved ones.

Energy!

Here is a sure strategy: to increase your energy, focus on results.

Focusing on results propels you forward because your very thinking about the results you want creates positive emotion which energizes you. (Read that again)

Positive emotion energizes you.

When I am writing, I focus on a) meeting my writing goals; b) the creative process of producing a book; and c) ultimately getting the knowledge of what I am sharing into readers hands and heads.

Focusing on these things energize me because of the positive emotion, or happy feelings, they create which causes me to keep acting effortlessly as far as energy goes.

On the flip side, if I focused on the writing itself, I honestly would never finish a project.

Writing is not for the weak. The process is difficult and takes a ton of time, self-control and self-discipline. Self-control to say *no* to yourself when you'd rather do anything but write and self-discipline to sit down and write when it's time to versus succumbing to unrelenting temptations pulling you to put it off.

The bottom line here is to keep your focus on results so you can leverage the energy it creates.

You need energy to be in your best state. You need energy to perform at your peak level.

You need energy to fulfill your life purpose.

Enthusiasm

Find and define your enthusiasm. What do I mean by this?

I am sure you have heard of a sweet spot. Figuratively, this is often used to describe the place where you are fully in and operating in your God-given purpose. Well, enthusiasm is similar to this.

To put it in simple terms, enthusiasm is "your thing." It is what you are into. What you love.

Different from passion — which is what you are willing to suffer for — enthusiasm is more like an interest that you are really into.

Like little boys are, by in large, naturally into collecting cars or baseball cards. Or like little girls are, by in large, into makeup and pageants, playing dress-up or the role of a mother with baby dolls and portable, play kitchens.

For some reason we lose this as adults.

And today, by and large (not everyone), we are increasingly allowing the snare social media to rob us of our pure interests by causing us to incessantly look at, compare and covet other things that are, most of the time, not even real life but rather facades that people are sharing.

Let that sink in and after it does get to work on identifying *your* enthusiasm. Define it and outline all the ways you can cultivate it.

Outside of the obvious – all things pertaining to self – my enthusiasm is productivity. After years of being the biggest procrastinator and never finishing a project I started, I am obsessed (in a healthy way) with the whole creative process from beginning to end.

And my actions show it. I read about productivity. I ponder it. I study it. I feast on it. I apply it to my life and business. I talk about it and I share my love and enthusiasm for it with others. I even look at it because I have productivity-related signs posted all around me in my workspaces, notes around my house, on mirrors, lamps, etc.

This is what enthusiasm looks like. Again, define yours. Start giving it some earnest thought. Really paint the picture. Go there.

Goal-Digger

Someone I used to work with had a sign on her desk that read "Goal-Digger." For me, this was love at first sight because an important tenet of my life is setting and achieving goals. Being a goal-setter and a goal-getter.

As you might gather, a goal-getter is someone who lives their life by consistently (keyword) setting goals and achieving them.

Before going any further, I want to bust the misconception that goals are limited to the typical thoughts about them — big personal and professional goals like family, education, entrepreneurism, corporate executive, etc.

A goal, no matter how small, can be made for any of the 5 major areas of our lives: self, health, relationships, finances and career.

Spending more quality time with your loved ones is a significant goal. As is controlling your temper. As is cutting back on sugar. As is sticking to a daily routine and developing more self-control.

What makes all these goals is not merely saying this or that is your goal, and not merely having good intentions toward them. What makes them goals is when you give careful thought to them (by asking the right questions); writing them out; and coming up with a *strategic* plan and action steps to execute your plan by a certain date. No matter if the date is near or far into the future. Serious goals always have a date attached to them.

Also, a key to making goals meaningful to you and your family, staff or stakeholders is making them *SMART: Specific, Measurable, Assignable, Relevant and Time-based.*

So, in other words, setting clear, meaningful goals where progress can be measured over time until the goal deadline is reached.

> *Setting goals is another little secret to self-control. They effectively cause you to be focused on something — which is where their secret powers lie.*

Now is a good time to recall the power of focus and the idea of energy blocks. When you are focused on something you are occupied, enthralled, all-in until you reach the end of it. You don't have time for anything else. You are focused. You are *in control*.

Ahh. Don't you just love the sound of that? I do.

My challenge for you here is to not just read this section and take no action. Rather, read this section and start to earnestly focus on creating goals (self-control and otherwise) for yourself. Set them daily and, if you're like me, throughout the day.

Currently, my serious self-control goal is to control my mouth; my speak. To be of few words all about quality not quantity.

Over the years, I've developed the habit to talking to myself and, while this is not necessarily bad in and of itself, there really is no virtue in it unless I am praying out loud, declaring the Word of God or reciting affirmations.

My goal when I speak is for everything I say to be impactful to the hearer. Whatever I speak, I want it to edify and not be idle. To be meaningful and matter greatly.

So, set self-control goals for yourself. Be just as passionate about small ones as you are about your big life goals. This is yet another way to be intentional in your personal development.

> "Work harder on yourself than you do on your job." Jim Rohn,

Grit For The Gravity Of Life

Admittedly, this might be a little corny at first but hang with me; I'm going somewhere good.

Will Smith, Hollywood blockbuster movie star, made a song entitled *"Get Jiggy With It."* It was an absolute hit. Why? The name was catchy — something that really sticks with you — and it had a nice beat. But the meaning people got from the lyrics is what really made the song catch like wildfire.

To be jiggy means to be jittery or fidgety. It is basically energy. Lots and lots and lots of energy.

As a play on this catchy tune, I want you to remember to *"get gritty with it"* when it comes to exercising self-control.

So exactly what will grit do for you?

Grit enables you to press in and through heavy obstacles.

To press through heavy obstacles, or what I refer to as the gravity of life. And not only press, but to do so with a sense of urgency. Not sluggishly but rather with energy from jitter-infused enthusiasm.

Enthusiasm has long been a go-to emotion of mine in various situations. If I am feeling nervous, I quickly change that story in my head and tell myself how excited and enthusiastic I am about whatever it is. If I am tired, same thing. If I find myself saying how tired I am, I quickly change the story and tell myself how much energy and enthusiasm I have.

Go with me here. Imagine a mover and he has a harness hooked up to himself and he has to move a load. He's walking and pulling that thing. He's having to *reeeally* press in — to really give it all he has— in order to move through the resistance he is walking through. To get through the force of gravity.

Do you think this mover would be able to pull this load in a significant way if he wasn't doing it with oomph? With nerve? With urgency? With gusto to get it done as fast as he can? Of course not.

Well, life is gravity and the gravity of life will threaten to hold you back, to keep you stuck, to shut you down and prevent you from fulfilling your maximum potential and purpose if you don't use some grit and press in to it. To "run into the roar" as NY Times bestselling author, Mark Batterson, would put it.

Balance

I would be sorely remised if I did not include the importance of balance in a book about self-control.

In the midst of all the striving to *be* and *do* to the end of self-control, there must be rest. I know most people don't like to think about, let alone talk about, but death is an equally beautiful part of life.

Death of our physical body is the guarantee of total liberation from our labor and toil. Freedom from every human striving to be this or that, achieve this or that, overcome this or that struggle, prove this or that, and on and on.

However, most people don't see it this way because the fallen mind of man has perverted the truth about death and made it something to be feared — ultimately because of unbelief in the existence and superiority of the unseen world and power and future paradise. And, because of the big role crime and vice plays in being a frequent perpetrator of death.

But I digressed.

Back on subject, know this. That our current physical bodies constantly yearn for rest— in the background, so to speak, even when our energy and enthusiasm is high — because they were made for permanent rest. Rest is essential for mental and physical health and well-being, which is our real wealth far above anything we can achieve and/or obtain.

When we lack adequate rest, any trace of self-control we might have dips and disappears quickly.

In the same way stress, frustration, hurt, anger or any negative emotion triggers out-of-control behavior, inadequate rest is also a trigger for it.

Scientifically, fatigue has an adverse effect on your thought processes, memory and learning which then leaves you in a position of straining to function and respond normally.

Further, research shows increased activity in our amygdala, which regulates emotions like anger and rage[1]. Hence the grouchiness when we are tired. When left unchecked, lack of rest carries the potential to turn into something much more serious.

Notes

[1] Journal of Applied Social Psychology. W. Christopher Winter, M.D., medical director of the Sleep Medicine Center at Martha Jefferson Hospital.

CHAPTER 9

Your Greater-Than-Self Perspectives: Drawing Out Deeper Meaning

As much as we tend to believe and continually convince ourselves – beginning at adolescence into adulthood – the truth is we don't know as much as we like to think we know and we're not always right. If you are honest with yourself, you will have little trouble admitting this. If you are both honest and humble, you will also have little trouble earnestly considering perspectives outside your own.

In the brief, few sections that follow, I am going to get a tadbit personal and go beneath the political correctness waterline and touch on some topics that are today talked about less and less as humanistic beliefs abound more and more in hearts and minds.

I must go here because self-control has depth to it. It is multi-dimensional.

We need it in order to feel and act our best; to treat ourselves and others well; to have healthy relationships; healthy finances; to fulfill our purpose; and to be open and sincere about learning what we don't know and, more difficult, accepting a truth that disagrees with our self-indulgent beliefs and behaviors. It takes self-control to draw out and assign deeper meaning to our own selves, perceptions and experiences. Otherwise, we tragically live shallow, non-chalet, self-centered and self-destructive lives.

12

I am a huge numbers girl. I have always found the meanings attached to numbers fascinating. It adds so much interest to life.

The number 12 is my life number. Biblically and otherwise, it is the number that represents governance and the number of authority. Governance and authority over every aspect of self and life from a power that is wholly outside, higher and greater than yourself — which for me is God, whose name is Yahweh, and faith in His Son, Jesus Christ.

What does this have to do with you and self-control?

Whether you realize it or not, something is governing your life.

There is an unseen power operating in your life that you are submitting to, and I challenge you to consider this and identify what power is potentially governing your self – your thoughts, hence, your actions. Could it be the grip of fear, unforgiveness, anger, addiction, hurt, hatred, rejection, resentment, bitterness or pride? Many in this list? All the above? Or something else?

Reward

There is great reward in sacrificing self (self-control) and waiting.

When you don't give in to getting what you want when you want it, but rather press-in to do what you ought to do or press-in to not do what you ought not to do, you can rest assured on reaping glorious rewards for it later.

In fact, in sacrificial waiting, the positive emotion you experience later will be even greater. Because it won't be from a fleeting "quick fix" gratification act. Rather, it will be the authentic satisfaction your soul is really searching for.

The law of sowing and reaping will see to it.

When you honor thy self, thy self will honor you.

I am a living, breathing testimony to this truth as I continually honor my body and make it the largest area of my worship to God; and, consequently, experience supernatural health, well-being and wholeness that is on a level so high I could have never thought or imagined it for myself.

While exercising self-control feels funky (i.e., uncomfortable) to our flesh, the results and rewards are worth every bit and then some because they lead to long-term fulfillment and satisfaction versus temporary fleeting gratification.

True fulfillment and satisfaction keep you healthy and well physically and mentally.

How so? With the positive emotion (happiness defined) and the energy they create. Both serve as a source of fuel for motivation.

Read that last paragraph again and let the church say *amen*. Just these two things alone are worth their weight in gold. Because you absolutely need a positive attitude and an abundance of energy in order to experience and enjoy life to the fullest and, moreover, to carry out your purpose.

If these alone aren't enough, here are a few other significant rewards of self-control:

1. **Freedom.** Freedom from the struggle and ills of self thereby enabling you to evolve into your highest and best self.
2. **Peace.** True inner peace because you have or are in the process of confronting and overcoming the root causes of out-of-control behaviors, bad habits and/or addictions and the fruit of the self-control strategies you are executing is beginning to bud.
3. **Power.** Power to fulfill your maximum potential by your actions because you are now empowered to *make good choices* every time.
4. **True satisfaction.** Not only because you are starting to experience more inner peace, but because you are not experiencing fake temporary gratifications. The choices you are now making due to increasing self-control result in authentic happiness and satisfaction.
5. **Energy.** Bad habits and out-of-control (ooc) behaviors consume and drain you. Bad habits are bad for a reason. They are detrimental to your physical and mental health because of their negative (toxic) energy and negative physical effects that either slowly chip away at you or cause massive immediate destruction depending on the

severity of the habit. When you do something ooc, you usually feel miserable a few hours later. High, hungover, angry, ashamed, etc. The inevitable crash when the high from whatever you did wears off.

6. **Extraordinary joy.** No longer being weighed down by heavy burdens, your whole being is lighter and you will naturally begin to be more grateful, which will cause you to naturally see beauty in people and things all around you. You will naturally seek laughter. With all these things combined, you will experience extraordinary joy.

Religion

In addition to being a huge numbers girl, I am also what some would refer to as "a holy roller."

Yep. I am *that* girl. I just love God. I love theology. I love the Bible and I love to study it. I love the Church. I love going to church and being at church (I could easily live there). I love God's laws and commands, and I love pushing my *self* to obey them. I love religion too – true, pure, undefiled religion. Not dogmatism and division through dominations. Not hypocrisy and not self-righteousness.

Humbly, this is who I am. Moreover, this is who my Maker made me to be, and I am neither fearful nor shy about sharing it with anyone in any setting, situation or circumstance.

Frankly, I have found and keep finding the longer I live in fear and obedience only to God and His ways, and not to Man and his ways, there is no better way to live in total victory in this present world.

I know religion has a bad rap.

Mainly because the religious man has made his religion repelling for people with his self-righteousness, hypocrisy, ill-judgment and condemnation of irreligious people not like himself — which you must know is *not* godly and at the extreme opposite end of the true nature and character of God Almighty.

In and of itself, true religion as God intended it is actually a very good thing.

Without getting deep because this is not the place for it, let me just say, on the upside, religion does a couple major things for us in the context of increasing self-control:

1. It begets humility by causing us to acknowledge the reality of and reliance on something divinely higher and greater outside of ourselves.
2. It *creates* self-control and self-discipline in us.

So, in this spirit, let me ask you: what do you fear in the sense of reverence? Consider sacred? Consider holy? Worthy of worship? Whatever this is and looks like for you, it will serve you well to apply this same school of thought to how you treat your own self and body. When you do, self-control and self-discipline will abound.

Providence

What I want to help you see here in closing out Part A before transitioning into Part B is this: that despite all your frustration, you are divinely right where you are supposed to be because of this notion called divine providence.

Hear me on this. Everything going on in your life is happening for a good reason. Not just happening for a reason but happening for a *good* reason. It will ultimately (keyword) work together with everything else past, present, and future to make you better in every way. To transform you into your highest and best self.

> *There is something in you that needs to be addressed and the situations and circumstances of your life are working to address them despite what it seems; despite what it looks like or feels like.*

All the pain, fear, frustration, stress, worry, anxiety and anger you are most likely currently experiencing is all part of what will ultimately be a victory song for you.

Remember one of our fundamental breakthrough thoughts; that pain strengthens. It is necessary.

Receive this truth and trust the process of *until*. That is, these things must be *until* your breakthrough happens in the perfect time. Press in to use your faith to dispel doubt and to believe the truth I am sharing here *until* they become a reality in your being and life.

Know that your breakthrough will happen for you, just like it happened for me and many other overcomers. We are living testimonies and you will be too. Hang on and be encouraged *until*...

Say this aloud: *everything is working for my good.*

The X Factor

Allow me to present some final food for thought as we transition into the next part of this book—the X factor. The unseen.

Whether you believe in the unseen or not does not negate the reality of it. It is the Spirit that gives life. The body is dead without the *breath* of life. Which, by the way, is unseen.

Let me prove it to you.

Go with me here. You are walking along in the park and you see a dead bird. The physical body of that bird is there but there is no life in it because there is no breath, or spirit, in it.

The same is true with a human being and human body.

No spirit. No life. Dead body. End of story.

Also important to note and for you to see/realize/get revelation of is that the unseen spirit world is superior to the seen physical world.

A spirit can exist without a physical body but a body cannot exist without a spirit. (Read that again until it sinks in).

Further, as it relates to thoughts, your thoughts are not a part of your physical body. You have never and will never physically touch one of your thoughts. They are unseen yet are very much yours and a part of you. The same with words. They are breath. Spiritual.

From these little golden nuggets, do you see the truth that you are much more than meets the eye? That you are more than a physical body? That you are a triune being — spirit, soul and body?

All this said, understand there is a spiritual aspect to self-control and specifically why your physical self might be ooc (if the shoe fits).

You have already learned — and hopefully accepted — the fact that you have the capacity within you to exercise self-control. There are just some things that need to be dealt with (destroyed) and some other things that need to be developed in order for self-control to surface and abound.

Now, then, let's keep the momentum going and get into *the work.*.

Part B: *The Work* of Transformation

Building Your Self-Control Through 50 Powerful Strategies

INTRODUCTION

Being strategic is fundamentally two things: thinking strategically and acting strategically.

In Part A, my intention was to share knowledge to get you to think strategically. In this second part of the book, my intention is to get you to act strategically.

Since this is a simple study on self-control versus a deep discourse for academic or professional disciplines, one of my main goals in Part B is to not bog you down with more thoughts. That is what Part A was for.

Here, I have included 50 one-word action strategies that are easy to apprehend, act on and remember. The intention for the strategies being presented this way is to:

1. *Leave space for you to apply the strategy to your self and situation/circumstances.* Space needed to be left for you to engage and wrap your thoughts around these strategies absent of a lot of ideas and opinions from myself and other works cited. This way, your self-control will begin to develop in a pure, natural, organic way that is authentic for what your needs are where you are.
2. *Be referenced often.* When developing self-control, repetition in thought and action is vital. Research shows, reading and acting on something over and over and over again increases learning (knowledge) and recall (action).
3. *Allow for quick reference.* The format and fonts (big and bold) lend themselves to quick thumb reference at any given time, particularly on-the-go when traveling, sitting in a waiting state or as light reading over breakfast, lunch or dinner.

Hopefully these intentions make good sense and will prove highly effective throughout this process for you.

Noteworthy

Before diving in, I want to note the following points for you to keep in mind as you read and, moreover, *work* your way through the 50 strategies. This is so you know exactly where I am coming from in general or for any given strategy.

- While I took some care to group similar, relatable strategies together, they are randomly ordered and not ordered by importance or any other significant association.
- Some (many) of these strategies will resonate with you but some will not — in which just skip over it and keep going through them. You may not need help in that area but someone else may. There is something here for everyone so just keep that in mind while taking these in.
- Feel free to read these strategies consecutively back-to-back (my personal recommendation for acquaintance sake) or thumb through them based on what your immediate needs are.
- These strategies are simplified language of scientific research-based concepts from psychology and positive psychology (the study of what goes right), and from the ancient wisdom of the Bible.
- You will notice similarities, commonalities, and some repeating thoughts between strategies. This is because they are designed to change your being for the better and repetition is a simple, highly effective way to do this.
- You will notice some strategies are short and sweet while others are longer (by necessity). Either way, they are all kept simple with space for you to go deeper with them if you choose to.
- There is an accompanying exercise at the end of each strategy. **Please, I beg of you to take the time to engage and *do the work*.** Have a pen and possibly a notebook/journal handy if you

don't feel comfortable writing in the book for whatever reason. The critical thing is to, right now, decide that you are going to do the work. This book is a *tool* for you and tools have zero value unless they are used. But when they are used, they get the job done. Commit to doing the work.
- On a personal note, I am presenting you with "strategies" and not "ways" or "actions" or "plans" because when you have an enemy (i.e., your struggle), you must be strategic in order to defeat that enemy. As such, something I often say to myself aloud as a trigger for exercising self-control is, *the devil got strategies, I got strategies too!* Feel free to adopt this as a trigger for yourself. It is definitely not proper English but who cares when it works.

Finally, one of my favorite quotes of all time and an excellent mantra to live by is from the legendary Jim Rohn, one of the first fathers of the Self-Improvement genre.

> "Don't wish it was easier, wish you were better. For things to change, you have to change. For things to get better, you have to get better!" —Jim Rohn

I love this because it is truly something to live by. Now let's get you to doing *the work* for breakthroughs, transformation and new life.

Strategy 1: Accept

*Be strategic and **accept** where you are today.*

In Part A we learned that acceptance is paramount when it comes to personal transformation. Because what acceptance really is, is facing the truth and accepting it, and thereby shutting down any delusion or falsehood that threatens to keep you stuck where you are. This is vital because truth is the only thing that truly liberates you. Knowing truth and accepting it.

Use the space below to tell yourself the truth and accept it. This is also the space to write out how you resolve to move forward in your thinking and actions.

_____

_____

_____

_____

_____

_____

Strategy 2: Embrace

*Be strategic and actually **embrace** where you are today..*

This strategy is the next level beyond acceptance. It is for those of you who already know truth and accept it and now have the opportunity to embrace it as something that is actually working for you and not against you — no matter how difficult, sad or bad the situation may be. Embracing is making a choice to see things differently. To see your current self, situation and/or circumstance through a positive lens and thereby shift the energy from negative to positive. Thus, as you move onward and upward it will be less of a struggle. The positive energy will propel you forward.

Use the space below to describe what it would look like to actually embrace your current plight as something that is actually working *for* you and not against you.

_____

_____

_____

_____

_____

Strategy 3: Examine

*Be strategic and **examine** what behaviors occupy the biggest place in your heart.*

Having self-control in abundance or not ultimately boils down to being a heart issue. Because of this, it is essential to examine your heart to see where your affections are. If your affections are set on physical gratification of any and every kind whenever, wherever and as much as possible, you will not be able to exercise self-control. In fact, the very thought of it will offend and repel you. However, if your affections are otherwise set on becoming something brighter and higher, increasing in strength of character and bodily virtue through the means of self-mastery, you will exercise self-control and increase in self-control. It is all about where your affections lie.

This strategy is vital to having more self-control. Challenge yourself to really open your heart and mind and go beyond reading over these words once.

Meditate on this strategy and examine your heart. Then use the space below and on the following page to write your hope for your heart in the context of having more self-control.

_____

_____

Strategy 4: Dig

*Be strategic and **dig** deep to identify the root of your behavior.*

Keeping first things first. Before you can make any significant behavioral changes that last and lead to genuine transformation, you must first become aware of why you are behaving as such. Why? So you can pluck the root of the rotten fruit. You can't conquer what you don't confront and liberating confrontation almost always involves replacing lies with truth. Self-control stems from thinking and acting based on truth.

Use the space below and on the following page to:
1. Identify "the event" (that is, a single experience or series of experiences or even something that did not happen that you needed to happen like receiving love) that caused you hurt and/or harm.
2. Identify the meaning you assigned to the event.
3. Answer the question of if the meaning you assigned to your event is actually *true*. If it is not true, state what *is* true.

_____

_____

_____

Strategy 5: Decide

*Be strategic and **decide** whether you are ready and willing to do what it takes to have more self-control.*

Here is the key, two-part question for you to answer:
1. Are you <u>willing</u> to exercise self-control, OR...
2. Are you <u>not willing</u> because you want to keep doing what you are doing because a) you enjoy it; b) you don't feel too bad about it; and/or c) you are not ready to give it up? Which would be ok. The important thing here is to locate yourself. To find out where you are then act accordingly.

Use the space below to decide to either commit to, completely can, or temporarily shelf the exercise of self-control. If you decide to commit, there are a couple more decisions you will need to make. They are:
1. Decide to deny your self of some indulgence on a regular.
2. Decide to be ok with feeling uncomfortable while building your self-control muscles.

_____

_____

_____

Strategy 6: Edit

*Be strategic and **edit** the story you have been telling yourself.*

To edit is to correct. To improve. To make better. To perfect (not be perfect, but to perfect as in improve upon as much as possible). As learned earlier, you are your thoughts because you cannot separate yourself from your thoughts. This is the very reason why your thoughts determine your actions. *Ultimately, you are your thoughts.*

So, then, the big question is what are you thinking about and is it the right way of thinking? If your behavior is out-of-control, your thinking is probably incorrect — whether consciously or unconsciously.

Use the space below (if needed, there is more space in the back) to answer the following questions that will help you edit the story you have been telling yourself. First, think about the biggest area you struggle with self-control in. Now, answer these questions:

1. What is the story you tell yourself about this?
2. Is this story based on what is true or based on a lie?
3. If a lie, what is the truth?

_____

_____

_____

Strategy 7: Label

*Be strategic and truth **label**.*

Truth label is what I refer to as calling things what they really (keyword) are. Speaking the truth out loud and not just silently in your head. Calling, or labeling, things what they really are. This is so powerful because what you begin to do is literally shift energy atoms from negative to positive. Negative words carry negative energy and positive words carry positive energy. This is why calling someone out of their name or anything along these lines hurt so bad.

Here is an example of what truth labeling would like look:

> If you need to prioritize something, call what is not important *"unimportant."* Label it what it is. This will immediately disarm temptation to give energy to something that is unimportant.

Truth labeling tares down bad mental constructs and replaces them with truth. This is powerful on its own but it also ties into using your words because when you accurately label and speak to it, there is tremendous creative power/force in this.

Use the space below and on the following page to write out as many personal scenarios you can think of in which you can start labeling, or calling, things what they *truly* are. Truth label.

Strategy 8: Assess

*Be strategic and **assess** your strengths and weaknesses.*

This is vital and one of the first things you must do in your endeavor to have more self-control.

First, take the time to identify your strengths and weaknesses (StrengthFinders 2.0 from Gallup is a great place to start). Second, print and post them so they stay in front of you (this is really important). Third, study them for a few days or more and allow them to speak whatever they will to you in terms of your personal capacity; the reason why you do this or that; areas you should or should not focus on; or the best next baby step for you to take. This is basically an awareness-building exercise.

Use the space below to write down the strengths and weaknesses of your personality.

_____

_____

_____

_____

Strategy 9: Exercise

*Be strategic and **exercise** your strengths to get stronger in your weak areas.*

Exercise your strengths to strengthen your weaknesses. In doing this, you are quite literally developing your self-control muscles.

In due time, what will begin to see happen is, you will become stronger and more self-controlled then you were before in your weak areas.

How is that so? Because of a key principle shared earlier: focusing on and doing more of what is right (acting on your strengths) than focusing on what is wrong (acting on your weaknesses).

Use the space below to come up with at least 3 self-control actions you can exercise in your strongest area(s). Think easy, medium, difficult. Once you have these, come up with the duration for each level then start your exercises.

_____

_____

_____

Strategy 10: Battle

*Be strategic and **battle** against your opponent.*

In a pursuit to win against an opponent, knowing that opponent gives you a tremendous advantage. Not knowing your opponent is like throwing darts at a target in a dark room you've never seen or been in before. When it comes to self-control, your body is your biggest opponent. It incessantly demands what is bad for it. It betrays you with sickness and disease (think common cold). It dies.

Knowing and accepting the truth that your body is an enemy opponent of yours, there is a key decision that must be made before you are able to effectively engage in battle and win. Here it is, in the form of two key questions. Ask yourself and answer:

> *Am I going to ally with my body or am I going to battle it? Am I going to feed the sickness and disease it is prone to or fight against the sickness and disease it is prone to?*

Use the space below to list at least 3 different ways you can start battling against your body.

_____

_____

_____

Strategy 11: Deny

*Be strategic and **deny** yourself of that indulgence.*

Most people fail when trying to deny themselves because they have an all or nothing approach — which does have its place for effectiveness. But not here.

For developing (keyword) self-control, denying yourself of some indulgence or addiction is something that is best done little by little. Just like you conditioned your body to crave what it now craves by repeatedly feeding on it, use the same approach to reverse unhealthy cravings by repeatedly denying them.

Start your denial routine by skipping a day or time. Also, *schedule* a time to deny. Make an appointment with yourself at the same time you would usually feed to instead deny. The goal is to not give in to every single urge you have. This will begin disempowering them.

Use the space below to come up with your denial routine.

_____

_____

_____

Strategy 12: Endure

*Be strategic and **endure** through feeling uncomfortable when denying yourself.*

It is our comfort zones — the things we do that keep us feeling comfortable— that keep us stuck.

When you endure and don't succumb to the demands of your body, know and anticipate that, initially, it is going to yell and scream at you until you give in and feed it something it merely wants but is not needed nor *designed* to consume (make sure you catch that).

The not-so-good-news-but-not-bad-news-either is that, with this strategy, you are going to feel uncomfortable. However, the good news is the discomfort will eventually pass away. You just have to press through and endure those initial feelings of discomfort.

Use the space below to write out how you will endure when feelings of discomfort surface but you know are temporary and will pass.

_____

_____

_____

Strategy 13: Pause

*Be strategic and **pause** in the heat of your moment.*

There are few things of a practical nature that are more powerful than pausing when in a heated situation. Pause as soon as you feel yourself on the verge of any of the following states opposite of self-control: angry, anxious, upset, frustrated, feigning, fearful, full of worry, lonely, desperate, discouraged or disappointed to name a few.

Press the pause button on these and other negative emotions. What this looks like is to simply stop for at least 10 seconds (very doable). Next, to close your eyes and take a few deep breaths. These tiny actions will disarm whatever negative emotions and create the space for you to choose (keyword) to shift to a healthier state.

Use the space below to identify the unhealthy emotional states you find yourself in most often and the opposite healthy state(s) you will aim for after pausing.

_____

_____

_____

_____

Strategy 14: Affirm

*Be strategic and **affirm** yourself.*

This is one of the simplest yet powerful ways you can brand truth into your mind. To speak what is true over yourself and over every aspect of your life through affirmations.

The branding comes from seeing them and speaking them out loud often until eventually they remain at the forefront of your mind and you are able to recall and recite them every chance you get when you are not occupied with family or work responsibilities.

Use the space below to write down powerful affirmations that will, among a host of other things, increase your self-control.

_____

_____

_____

_____

Strategy 15: Act

*Be strategic and **act** by adopting Do It Now.*

If you need self-control to do something, use *Do It Now* as a trigger. Beneath the surface, *Do It Now* is all about acting out of a sense of urgency. Urgency to take action and keep taking action until you get your task done.

This relates to self-control because having a sense of urgency keeps you focused, which requires self-control. You cannot focus at length without exercising self-control in your mind and/or physical activity depending on what you are focusing on.

Also note, if you need self-control to abstain from something, reverse and *Don't Do It Now*. Actually tell yourself, speaking out loud, *don't do it now [your name]*. This is wildly effective as well.

Use the space below to write down things you have a habit of putting off until later but will now apply *Do It Now* (or the reverse).

_____

_____

_____

Strategy 16: Refocus

*Be strategic and **refocus** on doing more of what is right.*

Where focus goes, energy flows. Therefore, focus your energy and actions on doing more of what is right instead of focusing your energy on trying not to do something you don't want to do.

Research shows that focusing on building your strengths is more effective than focusing on fixing your weaknesses because a) your strengths are always with you and b) you are able to create situations where you can use your strengths to build self-control.

For example, if you want to stop eating so much don't focus on not eating. Instead, because you are great at multi-tasking, one thing you might do is focus on strategically filling your time/schedule with responsibilities and activities so you don't have time to overeat.

Use the space below to list out the right things you will focus on doing more of.

_____

_____

_____

Strategy 17: Identify

*Be strategic and **identify** your passion.*

In our world today where content of all kind abounds, there are words and phrases that get overused and as a result they lose their meaning and, more detrimentally, they lose their power. Such is the case with the phrase "identifying your passion" or some variation of this.

I don't know of a way to articulate how critical of a key passion is when it comes to increasing in self-control. The word *passion* in the Greek language means suffering so "identifying your passion" translates to finding out what you are willing to suffer for.

Personally, I've had head knowledge of this for many years, but it did not become a revelation until a few years ago when I noticed one day that I was right in the middle of suffering for my passion of teaching and training through writing.

A passion project gives you something to "jump" out of bed for (*Jump* is a self-control strategy we will get to below). Grinding will also keep your mind and hands busy thus keeping idleness at bay. It is true that an idle mind is the devil's playground.

So get a passion project and set SMART goals for it. Give yourself a deadline. Define your work boundaries and get your nose to the grind. Stick to it. Don't stop until you *finish* the project. The fulfillment you will experience will be so rich and satisfying that you will want to experience this feeling time after time again.

Use the space below to identify your passion – what you are willing to suffer for. What work are you being called to do around this?

_____

_____

_____

_____

_____

_____

_____

Strategy 18: Partner

*Be strategic and **partner** with your purpose.*

Realize you have a purpose box. The contents are assigned to you. You are the only one that can ever make use of your purpose box because it is a personalized set of tools that include your gifts, your talents, your voice and your unique personality to express your voice in a way that no one else can and in a way that the people you are called to serve will be able to receive your message.

Use the space below to a) make an inner vow that you will no longer neglect your purpose box, and b) write out ways you can begin to partner with your purpose straightaway.

TIP: Start small. When it comes to the beginning stages of fully operating in your purpose, baby steps are often the most significant.

_____

_____

_____

_____

_____

Strategy 19: Master

*Be strategic and work to **master** some aspect of your self.*

A lot of ground has been covered so far and it really all comes down to one question that you must a) answer and b) act upon when you have your answer.

This imperative question: w*hat are you committed to mastering?*
Self-control is the fruit of your core being, or your character. It (or lack thereof) is a natural result of who you are.

Now don't misunderstand me. My last statement is not to say that if you lack self-control than you lack character. We know there are other complex factors and influence – such as hurt, mental health issues, illnesses, instability, addiction, and so on – that must be considered with respect to capacity and the exercise of self-control. What this statement does mean is, self-control is a natural consequence of noble character unencumbered (whether you accept this truth or not).

As I shared earlier, and well worth repeating over and over again, whether you know it or not, or are willing to accept it or not, we are all either mastering something or being mastered by something.

Admittedly, while this sounds a bit monstrous, and as tempting as it may be because of it, don't let the idea of mastery intimidate you. The key is to start small and mature over time. Because, contrary to popular opinion and culture, success does not have a size and mastery is not monstrous. It simply needs a decision, a commitment, and consistency in order to exist and abound.

For example, you may choose to master the habit of writing every day. Or reading every day. Or meditating every day. Or eating 5 servings of fruits and vegetables every day. Or drinking 8 cups of water every day. Or walking or running a mile every day. Or extending kindness to someone every day. Going to bed/getting up early...

Whatever you choose, make sure you do it every day to begin reversing whatever vicious uncontrolled cycle you currently feed everyday (e.g., smoking or overeating). Lastly, in developing mastery, remember the *Refocus* strategy that focuses on building your strength in order to eventually overcome weakness.

Use the space below to write what you are committed to mastering.

_____

_____

_____

_____

_____

Strategy 20: Obsess

*Be strategic and pick something good to **obsess** about.*

Ever heard of a guilty pleasure? Well let me introduce its polar opposite: *healthy obsession*. With this strategy, I want to challenge you to pick something good to get obsessed about. Some thing or some mindset that moves you closer from where you are to where you want to be.

You want to lose weight? Get obsessed with saying no to unhealthy, frequent food cravings. You want to stop smoking? Get obsessed with the feeling of gratification you get when you don't give in to having a cigarette. You want to have more self-control in general or something not listed here? Get obsessed with feeling uncomfortable for an initial period of time, knowing that the ultimate feeling of empowerment will be beyond worth it. What you are after is the actual *feeling* of empowerment, the opposite of the feeling of defeat you feel when you don't exercise self-control.

Right now, I am currently obsessed with 3 things: purity, finishing and arugula. For purity, not in a chastity sense (although that applies too), but purity in everything from the beverages I drink, to body soap, to all-natural deodorants and fragrant oils, household items, clothing, etc.

Any and everything must pass my purity inspection in order for me to touch it, consume it, use it, wear it, be around it, engage with it or whatever the case. Finishing projects is a big driver for me right now because for so long I started projects and did not finish them. I have a lot of time to make up for. And on a funny note for all my foodie's out there, I am now and forever will be obsessed with eating raw arugula. This has been a healthy obsession of mine daily for the past 5 years and counting.

Ongoing healthy obsessions I have are giving financially to worthy causes, productivity and (can you guess the last one?) self-control, of course; particularly, when it comes to conditioning my body and what I consume. I'm totally obsessed with these.

Use the space below to consider a new healthy obsession and color in a few details of what your actions will be around it.

_____

_____

_____

_____

_____

_____

_____

Strategy 21: Substitute

*Be strategic and **substitute** an unhealthy craving you are having with something else satisfying.*

Recall through transmutation you are able to shift your energy from one thing to the other. So when you are contending with a strong urge to feed an unhealthy habit or craving, don't just automatically give in to it. Act on your ability to do something else healthy and not harmful that will satisfy that same urge. You just have to make sure your healthy choice is something that *truly* satisfies you.

For example, when I get an urge to eat something indulging and I know it's just an unhealthy craving for comfort, I will read or start working on one of my goals. Both of these things give me a great deal of satisfaction. If it is a stubborn craving that doesn't want to go away quick, I will eat a piece of garlic (an appetite suppressant) or opt for something to drink (fancy water laced with lime, basil and cucumbers, concord grape juice or pomegranate coconut milk).

With this substitution of an unhealthy habit for a healthy one that will also give a raw feeling, it is important to know your strengths (learn what yours are from any one of the *Strengths Finder* books or Gallup's online assessment tool). Because if one of your top 3 strengths is learning, then reading will give you the gratification you are craving. Or, if creativity is one of your top 3 strengths, writing a story, doodling, or whatever you do to create will be just as gratifying as the unhealthy habit would be.

Use the space below to identify as many healthy things you can come up with that bring you satisfaction. For example, my list would include writing; listening to music; reading/researching/studying; praying/meditating or dancing.

_____

_____

_____

_____

_____

_____

_____

_____

_____

_____

_____

Strategy 22: Immerse

*Be strategic and pick something to **immerse** your self in.*

Once you pick something good to obsess over, you need to take the right actions to make your new healthy obsession happens. Obsession is more the mental workout, or mental strengthening, while immersion is the physical work, or the physical strengthening toward whatever you are setting out to achieve.

What I love about immersion is the fact that it is being all-in. If you are not all-in, you are not immersed. Think of being water baptized by immersion. You go down and are fully surrounded. You're all-in.

When I need to fully immerse myself in something, I remind myself of a metaphor that came to my mind once and has never left. If I try to be halfway in and halfway out, it would be like mixing ultra-purified water with human wastewater. I know this is a bit gross but it gets the point across so well.

Even if you mix a tiny bit of wastewater with pure water it still taints the pure water to the point where it is no good. The amount doesn't matter at all. What matters is two opposites were mixed. Halfway in and halfway out are opposites that cannot be mixed.

Use the space below to write what you can immerse yourself in. If you don't currently have something, what can you create or start working on?

Strategy 23: Consume

*Be strategic and guard your gates. Be keenly aware and conscious of what you **consume**.*

The first thing I want you to remember for this strategy — from Chapter 4's section on *Intake* — is the fact that your intake is much more than food and drink. It is all sensory input. Any and everything you take in from any one of your five physical senses constitutes as intake. Primarily, what you see, what you hear, what you taste and what you touch (physical intimacy and any type of sex).

Second, I want you to really become a "beast" (translation: prolific) with this strategy. *You become what you feed on; what you consume.* Just like food makes us grow, the intangible things we consume also grow and get bigger until we eventually become that. Whether you are awake to it or not, know this: all parts of your being — spirit, soul and body — are being fed and being formed by your consumption. The question is if what you are feeding on is helpful or harmful to your health and well-being.

Consider your intake today and over the past week, then use the space on the following page to write down what you need to cut and what you need to consume more of.

Strategy 24: Jump

*Be strategic and **jump** up as soon as your alarm goes off.*

This strategy will give you the same result that taking a cold shower would: instantly get you going. *Instantly* being the keyword here.

From now on, when your alarm goes off, start telling yourself a different story. Instead of telling yourself things like *I don't want to get up; this bed feels so good; just five more minutes* (3-5 times at minimum); *I'm calling out today, etc.*, say to yourself, *yes! A new day and a new opportunity to be more; Today I am going to win; I cannot wait to help someone and be of service today; There is nothing for me laying in this bed but everything waiting for me when I show up* (one of my personal favorites), *etc.*

Jumping is all about telling yourself a different story. Remember, where the mind and mouth goes, the man follows.

This strategy is so simple yet so good, and one that works for me every single time. Having the discipline to get up early and with enthusiasm is something worth putting ample energy and effort into because it is probably the simplest, single-most powerful strategy you can do that has the greatest potential to completely transform your entire being and, consequently, other major aspects of your life.

TIP: Set your alarm to the loudest setting so it will really startle you. This way you'll jump up naturally. Then just stay up by telling yourself a great story, like how excited you are to take that first sip of coffee and take the day by its horns.

Use the space below to 1) write out the story you are going to tell yourself — starting tomorrow morning — that is going to make you jump up as soon as your alarm goes off; 2) detail how you are going to start your day on the right foot as a result of getting up on-time.

_____

_____

_____

_____

_____

_____

_____

_____

_____

_____

Strategy 25: Hydrate

*Be strategic and **hydrate**.*

When you are fighting an urge to eat or indulge in whatever your guilty pleasure is, get a drink of water.

As I shared throughout Part A, since our lack of self-control is often the result of feeling frustrated, anxious, stressed or some other unwelcome emotion, the fact is we are just looking for an outlet for this negative energy. Getting a drink of water instead of eating the entire bag of cookies or potato chips, or smoking a pack of cigarettes, or taking a hit will do the same thing in terms of diffusing the negative energy that is actually causing the overwhelming *just-make-me-feel-good-now* urge you are experiencing.

Now you and I both know drinking water and eating cookies (or whatever indulgence or addiction) will not give you the same feeling. However, the act of directing your energy to something more positive will not only work in terms of a diffusing strategy, but it will also be beneficial to your overall health.

Much of the time, our body is just experiencing dehydration but because we always want to feel good, we do whatever feels good in the moment regardless of whether it is harmful to our health. Enough of this and we not only become wrongly conditioned but, even worse, our brains become chemically addicted to cravings produced by raw feels.

Last but not least, hydrating will actually make you *feel* better. More alive, alert and agile. Water clears your mind. It improves sleep, memory, concentration and focus. It gives you energy. It's a bone strengthener. It's good for your cardiovascular health, digestion and many other benefits. Opt for the water. It is clearly the better choice.

Use the space below to write down your gut reaction to the nuggets of truths shared here. Going forward, what will you do differently?

_____

_____

_____

_____

_____

_____

_____

_____

_____

_____

Strategy 26: Survive

*Be strategic and only eat to **survive** during your work week.*

Challenge yourself to change your view of food. To change your mental model and start to look at it *more* as nutrition and survival and *less* as something that completely overwhelms your senses in *every meal*. Yes, food should be enjoyed but only on occasion and not every single meal you eat. Put this in practice during your work week routine.

Notice I emphasized "more" and "less". Reason being, this is not to be something strict and rigid like law. There must be balance. And it is a fact that food is something that God provides us with in abundance to be *enjoyed*. That being acknowledged, like so many things, our wonky human nature goes overboard and starts to misuse and abuse something that in and of itself is very good.

When you start first start feeling hungry, stop telling yourself the story that you just must have something to eat *now*. What if there was a famine in the land? Or a situation arose where food had to be rationed? If we are honest with ourselves, we will admit that we eat too much and over-rate food. Yes food is yummy, but once you're done eating, a lot of times you think, *it was alright.* Basically, we hype it up to be much bigger than what it is because we have over time a) conditioned our bodies to eat even without being scientifically hungry; b) habit; and c) now we have an appetite that is constantly demanding food because it is constantly being fed.

What this issue of eating really boils down to is we are really trying to fill and nurture our spiritual need with physical substance. As hard as we try (i.e., as much as we eat), it does not work! And it never will! Jesus said, that which is spirit is spirit and that which is flesh is flesh. Your spirit — the superior part of you — must be fed with the Bread of Life from heaven not bread from earth.

Use the space below to plan your "survival" meals during your next work week.

_____

_____

_____

_____

_____

_____

_____

_____

_____

_____

Strategy 27: Ration

*Be strategic and **ration** portions of food for yourself.*

To ration is to allocate a particular portion. In effect, what I am basically getting at here is portion control.

Not everyone, but most people, including myself, have at some point or another been guilty of eating an entire portion of something in one sitting. Particularly when feeling frustrated, stressed, pressed, upset, angry, aroused, hungry, tired, or you name it.

Why? The over-simplified answer is the incessant demands our bodies put on us to feel gratified at all times. So we have this enormously strong, overwhelming energy always tugging on us to give it attention in the form of some raw feel-good relief. Did you catch *always?* Always.

An effective way to not feed your body's unreasonable demands to gratify in the form of gorging food is to take a portion and put the rest back.

TIP: Eat slower during your next meal. Research shows when you eat slower you feel fuller faster. For you to increase self-control in this area, this must become a habitual not an occasional thing.

Use the space below to come up with a plan to ration your portions at home and when eating out. Do you not need to have something at your disposal altogether? Do you need to place it in an inconvenient place or make getting it inconvenient? Do you need to keep something frozen so by the time it thaws out you are over it? Really give this strategy some strategic, creative thought and come up with your own questions. Remember, when you ask the right questions, you get the right answers!

_____

_____

_____

_____

_____

_____

_____

_____

_____

_____

Strategy 28: Fast

*Be strategic and **fast** at the same time every week.*

If you don't know, fasting is simply abstaining from food for a certain period of time. Among many benefits, you give your digestive system a break. If you are like most and tend to eat worse on the weekends than during the week, Monday's would be a great day for fasting. Because, again, people usually "go-in" on the weekends after exercising more discipline during the week. Too, fasting increases your strength in self-control because you are abstaining. It also increases your focus on more important matters as a byproduct because while fasting you are not distracted with indulgences.

Use the space below to outline your new fasting routine. What day you will fast? How long you will fast? What you will fast from and what you will fast *to* (that is, what you will do in place of what you would normally do but are fasting from)?

_____

_____

_____

_____

Strategy 29: Be

*Be strategic and just **be**.*

There is a phrase that, surprisingly, became a catalyst for transformation for me. The short, simple phrase: *let it be what it is.*

Absent of any intention, I found myself saying this during times when I would feel stress and frustration coming on and, consequently, felt urged to act or react based on outside influence (which, by the way, is *not* what you ever want to do especially when your goal is self-control).

Terri, let it be what it is, I would say to myself out loud. *Just let it be what it is.*

I have found this phrase to be extremely disarming. After speaking these words once or twice, I am literally able to let go whatever negative emotion and urge to act out of that emotion and instead enter an authentic state of peace and *being* still.

It is quite amazing and equally powerful. Because, in essence, what this really is is surrender. I hope you see that.

Naturally, we are independent doers and performers. Men and women in very different ways but both doers nonetheless. From birth, we are conditioned to *do*. Some things fnecessary and practical and some things purely out of ambition and the desire to excel and achieve – which, in and of themselves, are not bad things.

The ill aspect of doing that we need to be aware of is doing and striving in order to compensate for not being whole. Too, the stress of life adds to our ill-doings because, by default, to alleviate the stress we end up running to the rawest of raw feels that are ultimately detrimental to our health and well-being.

Now is a good time to recall one of our key breakthrough thoughts — we are not whole on our own, thus we are always striving to *feel* whole. With this, realize that striving is the opposite of being. One is consciously doing the other is consciously not doing.

Use the space below to write what you need to *let it be what it is* so you can just *be;* to just *be* in order for peace and calm to overcome all stress, strain and striving.

_____

_____

_____

_____

_____

_____

Strategy 30: Brake

*Be strategic and pump the **brake** on being in a rush.*

One of the easiest and quickest things you can do to increase self-control is to slow down. To be intentional about going at a slower pace than normal for you. When you slow down, it is very deliberate and intentional and controlled (keyword) behavior versus going with the pace of your busy commute, your busy world and your busy life.

During your next commute, deliberately drive slow for the entire commute. Stay in the right lane on the streets and highway. Resist the urge to pass no matter what – even if you are behind a truck, school bus, or slow driver.

The key to being successful at this is you have to have the right mindset. You may want to play your favorite music or listen to some motivational audio. Do whatever it takes to get you self in a mindset of not rushing.

This will be a challenge at first and even feel uncomfortable. You *will* have to resist your urges to speed up, pass or what-have-you.

After you get through a successful slow commute, be intentional and do it again until you eventually get to the point where you have scheduled "slow days," which are days where you deliberately drive slow during your commute.

Use the space below to decide on your scheduled slow days and your mindset-shifting activities on those days.

_____

_____

_____

_____

_____

_____

_____

_____

_____

_____

Strategy 31: Thank

*Be strategic and **thank** instead of doing something else.*

Gratitude and self-control? Who knew.

The next time you have an unhealthy urge, eating for example[1], first pause.

Then, think about how grateful you are to have eaten a few hours earlier. Then, think about how grateful you are for what you have within your reach — food and other resources. Then, think about how grateful you are to have the option to eat whenever you want when so many in the world don't know when and from where their next meal will come, if it comes at all. Think about how grateful you are for the next meal you will have; how satisfying it will be because you waited and gave yourself time to build up true hunger.

Simply sit, and think, and thank instead of doing anything else.

Use the space on the following page to give thanks for what you are grateful for in this very moment. Don't hold back. Fill up the space!

---

[1] I used food for this exercise, but food can be replaced with any unhealthy urge. If it is a cigarette, instead of smoking, think about how grateful you are that you still have functioning lungs allowing you to breath. If it is alcohol, think about how grateful you are that your liver is still functioning to cleanse your blood. And so on.

Strategy 32: Speak

*Be strategic and **speak** affirmatively when it comes to your capacity for self-control.*

As hyperbolic as it sounds, the power of a dynamite explosion is in your words. Words have the power to build and destroy (what dynamite does). Know and accept the truth that there is tremendous power in your words to instantly shift your energy from negative to positive or vice versa.

With this, stop saying what you don't want because it has a major effect on you. Be strategic and say what you do want. Say what you should say that will cause you to start truly wanting (key phrase) what you are saying . For example:
- *I want to workout*
- *I want to eat a pear instead of pizza for breakfast.*
- *I want to limit my sugar and sodium intake.*
- *I want to get up with energy, enthusiasm, and excitement.*
- *I want to go to work and be of service to someone.*
- *I am financially well-off.*
- *My health and wealth comes from writing* (one of my personal declarations).

Come up with your own. Hide them in your heart as well as speak them to yourself often and out loud.

Think about what you are saying to yourself as it relates to self-control on a regular basis. Are you saying what you don't want or things that are not true? Things like, *I have zero self-control. I just can't resist. This one time isn't going to hurt me. I am in too deep. There's no hope for me so what's the point of quitting now? This is just what it is for me.*

The expected outcome of this strategy is to use your words to create positive energy in the area(s) you want to increase self-control in.

Use the space below to write the words and phrases you commit to speak over yourself every day for the next month and beyond.

_____

_____

_____

_____

_____

_____

_____

_____

_____

_____

Strategy 33: Peer

*Be strategic and **peer** into the past and peer into the future.*

Admittedly, this is somewhat of a weird word for a strategy because of its uncommon use, but it is powerful nonetheless.

To peer is to look keenly at something. So, with this strategy, when you find yourself in a heat-of-the-moment situation, use your oh-so-precious moment of decision to first pause. Don't make any moves outside of closing your eyes and taking a deep breath or two. Next, direct your thoughts these two ways:

1. Peer into the past. Recall how you felt after the last time you went there.
2. Peer into the future. Imagine how you will feel afterward if you decide to go there again.

With these, don't just have a quick thought. Paint the picture. Recall and imagine in vivid detail (key phrase) about the consequences of the choice you are about to make. To make this strategy even more effective in increasing self-control, after peering, ask and answer the following power question out loud, *what is the best possible action I can take for the self I see myself as?*

Use the space below to practice peering and list unwanted emotions you've felt in past heat-of-the-moment situations. Also list how you want to feel in future situations you might find yourself in.

_____

_____

_____

_____

_____

_____

_____

_____

_____

_____

Strategy 34: Imagine

*Be strategic and **imagine** good things.*

I don't have to tell you that your mind is powerful. It creates and colors your experiences in this world. Fundamentally, the quality of your being and life depends on the quality of your beliefs, intentions, thoughts and actions.

Too much of the imaginations of man (humanity) are used for evil. Decide to use your imagination for good. Use your imagination often (keyword) to:

- See the person you dream of and are becoming.
- See in detail how you want to and will act in a certain situation the next time you find yourself there.
- See yourself taking powerful action.
- Dream about your big goals and the steps you are going to take to get there.

There is a verse of a Psalm in scripture that starts out "O taste and *see* that the Lord is good..." I don't know about you, but I like the sound of that.

Go here with me. Find a quiet space to retreat to and do nothing for a few minutes. When you've reached a state of calm, start imagining yourself as the person you want to be and the life you want to live. Really paint the picture down to the smallest detail. See yourself there. Focus on your self. Your self-controlled self.

Use the space below to write out the thoughts and visions that came to you during your imagination retreat.

_____

_____

_____

_____

_____

_____

_____

_____

_____

_____

_____

Strategy 35: Listen

*Be strategic and **listen** to something profitable every day.*

I cannot stress enough the benefit of something good going into your ears. Your ear gate is one of two major gateways to your soul (the other being your eyes). This is important to know because your soul is the control tower for your mind, will and emotions — all of which determine your actions and, ultimately, your quality of life.

Ponder for a moment how much sound we hear on a daily basis. Staggering isn't it? Now, ponder how much of what you hear is actually beneficial to your health and well-being. Another staggering thought — but quite likely in the opposite direction.

Most of what we hear is noise and not profitable. Because of this, we must be intentional about what we allow through our ear gate and what and how often we intentionally (keyword) feed into it.

Another importance with this strategy is to consider the time of day. In the morning you may need to listen to something educational or motivational that will get you pumped and in the right headspace for whatever you will face that day. In the evening you may need to mellow down and listen to music that soothes your soul.

Listening to good music is always a good idea. But, with the exception of music lovers, most people only listen to music occasionally like at a special event; when needing to calm down or unwind from stress; or possibly while traveling.

Given how great it makes us feel, I am a strong advocate for incorporating music we love into our daily routine. Research shows music can be more powerful than medication because of its ability to dramatically reduce stress and anxiety by a) increasing positive emotion (a definition of happiness); b) actually decreasing pain; and c) stimulating the "feel good" chemical dopamine – just to name a few. There are many other positive effects music has on us.

Finally, with this strategy, I encourage you to press in and have some conviction about doing this consistently. Reason being, it is so easy for us to hop from one thing to the next as we go through the motions of our days and responsibilities. So we be very intentional about this to the point where it becomes a habit and not just a crutch you use every now and then.

Listening to motivational audio and music everyday has completely transformed my being, actions and outcomes. *#Powerful*

Use the space below to list your listening interests as well as plan the time(s) of day you will listen to what.

_____

_____

_____

_____

Strategy 36: Edify

*Be strategic and **edify** your spirit self.*

Unhealthy habits and addictions to a high degree are our attempts to fill our spiritual thirst and hunger with some sort of physical matter (such as money, social media sites, movies/entertainment, video games, infotainment, improper/illicit sex, codependency on people, possessions, etc.) or some consumable substance (such as food, artificial stimulants, alcohol, and drugs). All raw feels.

What we should do instead is feed our spirit what it is truly hungry and thirsty for: spiritual meat. You may choose to feast on the bible or some other spiritual book; a devotional; a blog post; a podcast, or whatever. The objective is to consume something edifying to your spirit. When you do this consistently, self-control will abound.

Use the space below to list things you can and will start consuming to edify your spirit.

_____

_____

_____

_____

Strategy 37: Read

*Be strategic and **read** something interesting or something related to your career, passions and/or purpose.*

Read and/or study something profitable and educational. Something that will increase your knowledge and, as a result, make you better in your being and doing. Something you are interested in. Something you have a passion for. Something that peaks and satisfies your curiosity. When we are learning, our positive emotion, or happiness, increases. This is a self-control strategy not only because it keeps your mind engaged and occupied but as your being increases and becomes better, better actions and outcomes are a byproduct.

Recent studies show, today, our senses are detrimentally overwhelmed from imagery. It is called Sensory Overwhelm. Graphical (too often, inappropriate) images from digital media outlets dominate our society today. Even at our workplaces there is no escaping imagery as presentations and other communication containing pictures and videos steadily increase.

Reading will bring much needed restoration and balance to your cognitive functions and increase self-control in the process by causing you to not being so bent on mobile devices and digital media.

Will you commit to becoming a learner? Learning is not only noble but it can serve as a catalyst to move you into your purpose because you will quite naturally begin to share what you learn with others.

Furthermore, this is an effective strategy because a) it keeps you busy and distracted and therefore out of trouble; and b) it increases self-discipline (your consistent actions) and self-control (your consistent character).

Use the space below to write down your list of things to read and/or study and the benefit in doing so. Also, make your commitment official by adding a starting date or timeframe to each one.

_____

_____

_____

_____

_____

_____

_____

_____

_____

_____

Strategy 38: Coach

*Be strategic and **coach** yourself by asking powerful questions in the heat-of-the-moment.*

When you ask the right questions, you get the right answers — which lead to right actions and outcomes. In the heat of a moment when you are struggling to abstain from something, get into the habit of asking yourself the right question(s) for that moment. Out loud.

Questions like:
1. *What is <u>the truth</u> about what I am about to do?*
2. *What is the best possible action I can take for myself right now?*
3. *If I do this, what are the consequences of my actions?*

Use the space below to come up with powerful questions to ask yourself that will result in the best possible actions and outcomes from heated moments of decision.

_____

_____

_____

_____

Strategy 39: Weigh

*Be strategic and remember and **weigh** what you want more.*

This strategy comes from what I call *The Principle of More*; weighing what you want more. Weighing is a powerful way to dictate our actions and, ultimately, our outcomes. In your next heat-of-the-moment situation, when you are faced with the choice to exercise self-control or not, weigh what you want more.

Speaking out loud, ask yourself this question: *Do I want _____ more or do I want _____ more?* Your answer will determine your action which will determine your outcome. Turn this into a habit and watch your self-control and your life skyrocket to the next level and beyond. You will live and experience life unlimited.

Remember what you want most then weigh this against your dominant actions today. Use the space below to write what your questions and actions will be in your next heat-of-the-moment situation.

_____

_____

_____

_____

Strategy 40: Slay

*Be strategic and **slay** your feelings.*

First, let me be clear and say feelings have their place. As humans we need to feel in order to identify with, connect to and love each other. This strategy is about not allowing feelings to come in when you need to be decisive and take immediate control in the midst of a temptation or bad situation.

Now, then, let's say you have found yourself facing a heated situation and the outcome hinges solely on you. In fact, absent of divine intervention, you are the only one that can resolve it because the conflict is between your spirit and your body. I don't have to tell you that human feelings/emotions kick into overdrive when under pressure. So exactly how do you handle yourself absent of feelings?

You go into what is well-known in the field of public relations as Crisis Management Mode, or CMM, where — because stakes are high when dealing with public figures — feelings are not allowed. Only quick, often times on-the-spot, matter-of-fact decision making to resolve the situation at hand to protect the name/reputation of the person represented. In this case, you. Your name and reputation.

Developing the ability to jump right into CMM in a heated situation with yourself will increase your self-control because it extinguishes feelings. No longer will you automatically succumb to raw feel urges to flip your lid or the like. Instead, you will keep feelings at bay and say *yes* or *no* — yes to whatever is healthy and no to what's not.

Use the space below to practice being in CMM. Think back to a situation you've been in or anticipate being in. Summarize the key triggers and what your response will be.

_____

_____

_____

_____

_____

_____

_____

_____

_____

_____

_____

Strategy 41: Submit

*Be strategic and **submit** to the governing authority in your life and hold yourself accountable.*

Who are you accountable to and who has authority in your life to provide wise counsel and correction when needed? Is it God? Is it your spouse? Is it your pastor? A professor; a mentor; a best friend?

Submission increases your self-control because we always do better when someone is over and watching us. Being accountable to something bigger and something outside ourselves has a tremendously positive influence on our thinking thus actions. We become more thoughtful about what we do because it is no longer only about self and what self can do/get away with because "no one else knows."

Use the space below to list the accountability in your life. If you currently have none, list names or roles for who you will seek to be accountable to as a result of putting this strategy into action.

_____

_____

_____

Strategy 42: Correct

*Be strategic and course **correct** when you get off track.*

There are two aspects of correction that I want to bring forth here. The first being inevitable moments of weakness, or vulnerability

Know that when self-control begins to abound in you, moments of weakness will happen. Expect them. Why? Because we are imperfect humans with fallen natures that naturally crave unhealthy stuff.

With this important truth in mind, know that there may be times when you are too weak to exercise self-control. Life may hit hard and it knock you off your square. The result could be a minor, inconsequential binge or major relapse that could take days, weeks, months or longer to recover from. Just hope for and do your best.

The second aspect of correction is course correcting some area of self. Like correcting crooked mindsets and thus behaviors the moment you realize you've made a mistake.

If we are intentional and earnest about our personal development, and therefore honest with ourselves, we will acknowledge the fact that, as flawed human beings, we need to course correct *often* – and this takes humility.

SELF-CONTROL • 255

So what would course correcting look like in a practical sense? While working on the final draft of this book, I had to course correct when I caught myself saying over and over — really complaining — how I could not wait to be done so I can move on to my next project. With my own words I was weakening the work of my hands with negative energy from the words themselves and from the energy I was bringing to my writing sessions. I had to repent, or course correct, so I could produce my best work. In this simple example, it is easy to see how a bad mindset affected my words and ultimately my actions.

As soon as (key phrase) you realize you are starting to inch in the wrong direction, course correct. Pause. Verbally acknowledge the fact that you are inching out of control. This is vitally important so your energy can shift back to where it needs to be as soon as possible. Verbal acknowledgment will accomplish this almost instantly.

Your speak might start off something like this, *"wait a minute... what am I doing here? ..."* Remember what you want and what you don't want. Weigh what you want more. Edit the story you're telling yourself. Use your words to shift your mindset thus actions and, ultimately, your outcomes. Return to having a strategic mindset and start recalling the best strategies that work for you.

First, use the space on the following page to write your ideal mindset and subsequent actions that will cause strength to arise and enable you to correct when you go off course. Second, use the space below to correct any current mindset or behaviors that are not in alignment with the person you see yourself as and doing the things you see yourself doing.

Strategy 43: Detach

*Be strategic and **detach** from your viewpoints and perspectives.*

Let me first be crystal clear that I am in no way suggesting you turn away from your basic beliefs and values. My objective here is to encourage you to open your mind up enough to consider other ways outside of your own. To consider other viewpoints and perspectives on what works — in this case in particular, all the things I have shared up to this point on how to have more self-control. Because, with all due respect, if your existing viewpoints and perspectives — which determines your actions and, ultimately, outcomes — worked, then you probably would not need to be reading my book.

The truth is, as good of a job as our ego's do in convincing us that we have it all figured out, we don't. We know most of what we know because we have found it out to be true by experience. But realize we (you) did not start off knowing. There is still much for you and for all of us to learn and prove to be true. However, if we insist on what we think we already know, we will no doubt miss out.

Use the space on the following page to acknowledge any current viewpoints you hold but, honestly, not sure about and thus willing to detach from them and consider other viewpoints and perspectives.

Strategy 44: Rest

*Be strategic and be intentional to **rest** your body.*

I know I don't have to tell you how important rest is. When your body is not properly rested, your level of self-control decreases.

Scientifically, fatigue has an adverse effect on your thought processes, memory and learning, which then leaves you in a position of straining to function and respond normally. Further, research shows increased activity in our amygdala, which regulates emotions like anger and rage. Hence the crankiness (and road rage in commuters).

The keyword in this strategy is intentional. Between busyness and time not being on our side, we are always doing something. Even for holidays and vacations nowadays, you will often hear the phrase *I need a vacation from my vacation* because there was no real rest involved. One may not have been "at work" but he or she was still busy planning, preparing, packing, traveling and whatever else all in the spirit of rest but unfortunately not in the law of it.

Rest today not only takes intention but it takes discipline — which is in the family of self-control. Discipline to turn away from the myriad of distractions vying for your attention and completely tune out. No television. No media. No movies. No mobile devices. No games. No going here or there. Just resting for at least 5 hours straight.

Why 5? No real significance. Five is just the number of hours I put in and it also happens to be the number of grace which I find quite fitting for the topic of rest.

Use the space below to detail how you plan to incorporate rest into your routine. Be specific.

Strategy 45: Believe

*Be strategic and **believe** exercising self-control is better than _____ [you fill in the blank].*

Our beliefs are the foundation for which everything else in our lives is built upon — which is why it is so important that our beliefs are based on truth and not deception or personal or popular opinion. Self-control is a fruit of operating in truth.

With this strategy I want you to believe or begin forming a belief that exercising self-control is better than any indulgence or any uncontrolled behavior. The *effect* of self-control is better. The *consequence* of self-control is better. But here's the catch. With this strategy you can't just take my word for it. You have to first believe it for yourself then act in such a way that aligns with your belief.

Use the space below and the following page to write what you currently believe about your struggle(s). Is what you believe *true*? What is the truth? What do you need to learn of and start believing?

_____

_____

_____

_____

Strategy 46: Anticipate

*Be strategic and **anticipate** self-controlled behavior.*

Just like you tell yourself how great your indulgence is going to be, and you anticipate how "good" it will be because over time you have effectively convinced yourself of this by the story you kept telling yourself about it, flip the script and tell yourself how *truly* great and *truly* good you are going to feel when you don't give in to unhealthy indulgences that have a sad and bad aftermath.

And, take it a step further and actually anticipate how super-fulfilled, super-satisfied, super-achieved, super-accomplished and super-amazing you are going to feel when you succeed in exercising self-control. Lay it on thick!

Use the space below to write out the new story you are anticipating telling yourself when the urge to indulge strikes. Be specific. Paint the picture.

_____

_____

_____

_____

Strategy 47: Forgive

*Be strategic and **forgive** yourself when you mess up.*

One of the most damaging things you can do when trying to develop self-control in some area is beat yourself up when you fall short. Notice I said *when* you fall short and not *if* you fall short. If you have not already found it, it is guaranteed that you will fall short. However, in doing so, you must know and accept the truth that failure is inherent to success. Let me repeat that: failure is inherent to success. Let me remind you of why: because there must be a situation, a setting if you will, in which self-control is developed. Self-control is not something you obtain after one success in exercising it. It is something you *develop* over time — countless times of fail/success cycles.

You must also know and accept the truth that it is not about how much you fail, but that you have enough fortitude to try again and keep trying until you reach success. Use this phrase as a motivating motto: *Try until.* Say it aloud right now: *Try until. Try until ...*

Use the space on the following page to a) write a forgiveness letter to yourself; and b) make an inner vow to yourself that you will not beat yourself up when you fail to exercise self-control. Rather, you will remember the truth that failure is a necessary part of the process and you will keep going. You will keep *trying until. Trying until.*

Strategy 48: Finish

*Be strategic and focus on your big **finish**.*

This is such a powerful strategy and if you will develop an insatiable, unrelenting, on-fire desire to finish what you start, this single strategy alone will dramatically change your being and your life for the better. Because in order to finish so many other virtues have to be in play: decision, clarity, commitment, consistency, focus, determination, and perseverance to name a few.

What I want for you with this strategy is to always have something you are working toward *finishing*. When you are focused on finishing something, it keeps you focused as opposed to being idle or distracted with things that have no value and possibly even harmful to you or anyone else. When you are focused on finishing it keeps you enthusiastic and it keeps your self in control.

Use the space below to write down what you are currently or will be focused on finishing in the near future and/or beyond.

_____

_____

_____

_____

Strategy 49: Expect

*Be strategic and **expect** success in self-control.*

Expectation is a powerful thing. Better said, it is an attractive force. When you expect something bad to happen, 9 times out of 10 something bad is going to happen. Conversely, when you expect something good to happen, something good will likely happen.

Important to note, expectation is different from wishing about something. Wishing is not substantial. However, when you have a zealous expectation it is usually based on something substantial that is causing you to have that certain expectation. In reading and applying the knowledge and strategies in this book, you have already begun developing or increasing in self-control. *Expect* even greater.

Use the space below to write out the initial areas you are expecting to reach self-control success in.

_____

_____

_____

_____

Strategy 50: Celebrate!

*Be strategic and **celebrate** your new self and the life you are living.*

Think of the last celebration you were a part of. Was it a wedding, a birthday party, a ball game, a super bowl party, a night out with the boys or girls, or some other special occasion that was cause for celebration?

Remember the experience in vivid detail and remember yourself in the picture. Remember your mood. Remember how much you laughed. Remember the somewhat electrifying feeling you felt radiating throughout your being and body — which was positive emotion, which is the simple definition of happiness.

There is tremendous power in celebrating. In rejoicing. In choosing to be grateful and thus glad no matter what (key phrase). *Every* day not just on occasion. This is a self-control strategy that will give any self-serving indulgence a run for its money any day of the week. Because the high from authentic celebration is truly positive whereas the high from self-indulgence is masked as positive but in reality is negative and detrimental.

Effects from authentic celebration: 1) last longer; 2) enable you to think back and savor the experience, which produces more positive emotion; and 3) because you are feeling happy, you are absent of pressure, stress and frustration which are common triggers for urging you to engage in some unhealthy habit or uncontrolled behavior like overeating or an angry outburst.

So celebrate. Choose to celebrate for no other reason other than the present moment. For all of the blessings of your life. And if you happen to be going through a rough patch right now, then celebrate all the blessings of your past. All the great experiences you've had. Celebrate your next new season. Celebrate the person you are becoming. Celebrate the success of a loved one or someone you look up to. There is always a reason to celebrate. Look for it & celebrate!

Use the space below to write all the reasons you have or will have to celebrate and detail how you will start celebrating.

_____

_____

_____

_____

_____

_____

_____

_____

Part C:
Experiencing
New Life

Wake Up and Experience
New Life Every Day

The Purpose of It All: Understanding The Big Picture

So what is the purpose of self-control? Is it really just to deprive ourselves and be in misery and mean to everyone because you are feeling deprived all the time?

Of course not.

Self-control is for our highest good.

The highest good of our physical bodies, our overall health and well-being and for humanity as a whole.

These bodies of ours are wonky and want what is bad for them. Self-control helps us to be good and do good to ourselves and each other.

What's more, self-control in and of itself has a purpose. It is one of the major natural means by which individuals become the best version of themselves *in order to fulfill their maximum potential in order to ultimately fulfill their divine purpose — their supreme reason for being physically alive — in life for the greater good of mankind.*

Self-control is full of purpose and this is the big picture.

However, I would be remiss if I did not mention the fact that contained within this bigger picture is a smaller one. One that helps us understand our self-control shortcomings better.

The fact that this life is tough.

There is no shortage of struggle, trials and tribulations. And, because of this, so much of our lack of self-control comes from our hurts and our hang-ups from those hurts. Because of the pain we are in, we naturally seek temporary gratifications to make the pain go away so we can *just. feel. better.*

Am I right? Can you relate?

But bigger than these tears streaming down my face (and maybe yours too) is a God who loves you and a God that wants you to be free and feel better. To be your best and live your best life.

Friend, give your pain to God and stop fruitlessly trying to get rid of it with temporary fixes ("patches"). You can trust Him to handle it.

Though difficult, surrender.

For your healing and ultimate wholeness, earnestly *try until* to let go of what you want and/or what you think you should have right now. Truth be told, you don't have what you want and to continue wanting what you do not have is not only foolish (with all due respect) but unhealthy and harmful.

Redirect your energy on to something greater. Something more significant. Something outside of yourself for the greater good.

Trust God and His temporal and eternal plans for you. He knows your final outcome. Surrender and trust Him to lead you to it.

Self-control also means freedom.

Freedom from bad habits, abusive cycles, bondages/addictions and any kind of self-destructive behavior. Self-control leads to freedom from all the struggles of self that we have to contend with. Self-control is what begets our freedom and keeps us free.

Now then. My last challenge to you. It is a decision you must make. Choose to treat this like we treat most books — lay it aside and move on to the next one — or keep this book within reach and reference it often. Know that repetition for us is what practice is to an Olympic athlete.

Conclusion: What You Can Look Forward To

When you become self-controlled in your thinking and actions you experience life anew.

New space exists for you to be who you see yourself as and to do all the things you see yourself doing. You are like a bird let out of a cage, no longer captive and free to soar.

On a brief personal note, this idea of *new* excites me so much because one of the top things of a long list of what I love about placing my faith and hope in Jesus Christ, is the fulfillment of His promise of new, abundant life found in the Gospel of John 10:10.

The Greek word for *life* used in this bible verse is translated zoë, which means life of God – Who, by the way, one of His many attributes is self-control. Everyone who has faith in Christ receives zoë, the life of God on the inside of them! Sit with this thought so it has a chance to sink in because it is nothing short of awesome.

In more ways than one, living with self-control is truly the high life.

As it increases an elevation happens. Your very being ascends. The lower frequency activities and behaviors you used to engage in are replaced with higher frequency ones. Lower frequency raw feels that result in activities such as overeating, indulging in whatever feels good and is fun, easy and/or entertaining disappear and higher frequency desires to learn, study, create and slay in your life purpose surface.

In existing and operating on a higher level, you will experience authentic and lasting fulfillment that a fleeting raw feel could never offer. This is because you were in fact made for higher — which is the reason why you are frustrated (if the shoe fits).

Your core being longs to create and it is your personal responsibility to continually stretch yourself out of comfort and fear to this end; as well as to discover your purpose, operate in it, and overcome any obstacles from this rightful place of being and living.

> *Self-control bridges the gap between your lower and higher self. Between where you are and where you want to be.*

Trust that on the other side of your self-control — your sacrifice — is something uniquely beautiful and amazing just for you. Let this truth be yet another motivation to endure. It will be beyond worth it.

Also know this: when (not if) you fall short during one of your many attempts to exercise of self-control, to beat yourself up and decide to throw in the towel will more than likely be your first inclination. Resist.

Realize the truth that falling short is an equal part of the process of developing self-control. There has to be failure in order for there to be success. I repeat, there has to be failure in order for there to be success. Refuse to have a pity-party. Instead, pick yourself up and begin again working your strategy or strategies with enthusiasm.

Finally friend, while on your journey, call to mind often that the season of suffering that comes with developing self-control will end in glory for you. Stay encouraged and in eager anticipation for breakthrough.

Cheers to new life every day,

Terri Andres

Bonus Content

Congratulations! You've finished the main parts A, B and C of the book. I hope you got a lot out of it and will refer back as well as recommend *Self-Control* as a premium go-to resource for yourself and others. Thank you for your interest and support of my message and work. It has been a privilege and honor for me to share what I have learned and practice in self-control.

If I know right, I know you are left wanting more and are eagerly anticipating your "next". Eagerly anticipating freedom and fully being the person you see yourself as and doing all the things you see yourself doing for yourself, your loved ones and those you are called to serve. In this spirit, I decided to add this bonus content.

You've read two or three times now, *when you ask the right questions, you get the right answers.* This is one hundred percent true. Questions challenge you to think deeper about yourself and/or situation in order to really get to the heart of the matter.

Here are two seemingly simple questions that, if you answer them honestly and authentically, could completely change the trajectory of your life starting right now.

> ***Question #1:***
> *What truth do I need to admit?*
> ***Question #2:***
> *What am I really afraid of?*

Know this. That all uncontrolled behavior — whatever it is to whatever degree — is the rotten fruit of a bad root on the inside of you. Some falsehood, some fear, some hurt, some relationship void, some childhood abuse or neglect, some anger, some bitterness, some revenge, some unforgiveness, etc. Whatever it is for you need to be identified, uprooted and casted away. These are two powerful questions to ask to begin the process of accomplishing this.

It is the truth and only the truth that will reveal the pathway to permanent freedom from whatever is holding you hostage and causing faulty beliefs and self-defeating behavior.

Finally, fear and self-control are connected because fear causes you to act in ways you normally would not and those ways are usually uncontrolled and self-defeating.

I can honestly say, answering these two profound questions played a major role in setting me free from years of fear-based thinking about life, people, situations and circumstances. I am now on the other side living abundantly in every way, completely free from the grips and torments of fear, and all of its many manifestations. I sincerely want the same for you. Dig deep.

Appendix 1

12 Sacred Self-Control Truths

I encourage you to muse over and memorize these self-control truths. Being able to recall and speak truth in a heat-of-the-moment type situation can and often will make all the difference in the choice you *get to* make in that moment.

Truth #1	Self-control development is a duty of man for the greater good of mankind.
Truth #2	Self-control is doing the opposite of what you naturally want to do.
Truth #3	Self-control is more about being and less about doing.
Truth #4	Self-control is a 3-fold discipline of the mind first, the mouth second and the man third. Where the mind goes, the mouth and the man follows.
Truth #5	Self-control causes you to discern and accept that everything sold is not meant to be consumed.
Truth #6	Self-control enables you to stop feeding disease and to rather start fighting it.
Truth #7	Self-control increases or decreases with every thought and action. Every single thing you do impacts your self-control or lack thereof.
Truth #8	Self-control development does not require massive strength upfront. With showing up consistently, meager strength turns massive over time.
Truth #9	Self-control development requires patience, forgiveness and gentleness with yourself.

Truth #10	Self-control development requires a willingness to go through a season of discomfort as you consistently deny yourself of raw feels.
Truth #11	Self-control is strengthened by pain (discomfort) and weakened by pleasure (comfort).
Truth #12	Self-control carries significant inherent purpose that is far superior than your personal opinions and indulgent, raw feel preferences.

Appendix 2

Commitment to Mastery

This is where the rubber meets the road. You have finally arrived at the place for you to identify the area of self that you will commit to master and set it in stone by writing it down and posting it on your refrigerator, mirror, dashboard, whiteboard or wherever you will see it constantly.

> **TIP:** Start small in your biggest area of struggle. For example, if you desire to stop smoking, don't make the obvious commitment of quitting cold turkey. Instead, smoke fewer a day. Or better, skip a day altogether. Then build up to two days, three days, and so on.

Here are my recommended steps to do this but, by all means, do what you feel led to do to complete this commitment to yourself.

1. Go back and re-read sections that resonated with you most; challenged you the most; you wrote the most notes on, etc.
2. After reviewing, ponder your biggest area of struggle.
3. Make note of everything that comes to your mind now that you have finished the book.
4. Give yourself some space. Take a few days to exhale and receive whatever your thoughts and life will speak to you at this point (be on the lookout for random confirmations)
5. Return to this commitment page and complete it, copy it or cut it out, and post it.

6. Last but not least, celebrate yourself for getting to this point and EXPECT even more of the positivity that is already manifesting in your life (just knowing that there will be a little upfront pain/discomfort in the process). Anticipate it. Taste it. Work for it. Wait for it.

I _____ make a commitment on this day of _____ to commit to self-mastery in the area of _____, understanding that I am embarking on a journey that will be filled with highs and necessary lows but will ultimately get me closer to becoming my highest and best self in order to be the person I see myself as and do the things I see myself doing for the greater good.

_____

Signature   Date

Appendix 3

Decisions You Get To Make

Self-control is the resulting behavior of your root being. It stems from who you are at your core — your character. When you water and nurture your roots, good beautiful fruit automatically begins to grow out of the darkness and dirt.

These simple declarations, ultimately decisions, are a powerful way of watering your character. They are the words that correspond to decisions you *get to* make at any given moment.

Start a new healthy habit today by speaking these affirmations out loud over yourself and over your life daily and be amazed at your personal transformation for the better and abounding self-control.

- *I choose life over death*
- *I choose health over sickness and disease*
- *I choose love over hatred*
- *I choose humility over pride*
- *I choose unity over division*
- *I choose forgiveness over offense*
- *I choose calm over chaos*
- *I choose faith over fear*
- *I choose peace over frustration*
- *I choose sacrifice over self*
- *I choose wisdom over foolishness*
- *I choose compassion over self-righteousness*
- *I choose _____*

Appendix 4

A Conversation With Terri

The essence of self-control is applying what is right (truth) and good (wisdom) to your own self (mind, will, emotions and body).

If we were seated together at a table for two, enjoying a cup of coffee and having great conversation about best lessons we have learned about our selves and life up to this point, I would share the following with you:

1. *I've learned that I don't have to accept my own thoughts by default. That many times they are untrustworthy, unstable fallen, fear-based, self-centered and so on. This is one of the most valuable things I have mastered. Now, I masterfully choose what thoughts I keep and what thoughts I completely discard. Why is this so valuable? Because thoughts are not just thoughts; they reap consequences.*

2. *I've learned to move out of the way. This is cliché' but very profound if you can catch it. To become nothing. To not be a factor. To live at the end of myself. To literally become nothing so God my Creator and Maker, whose power is at work in me (and at work in you if you allow Him) can work perfectly without interference or disruption from me. Because I tend to mess up and get things wrong.*

3. *I have learned to say NO to unhealthy cravings. To just say no. Listen, the cravings are going to come. Just say no to them and keep moving.*

4. *I have learned that focusing on mastery in one area transforms my entire being. One area of mastery positively in-*

fluences other aspects of my life — service, self, spirituality, health, wealth, relationships, and career.
5. I have learned to see situations from other perspectives outside of my own. First God's. Then others. Then my own.
6. I have learned to, when I first wake up, to tell myself the story that will make me leap out of bed in the morning. To get on about the day with passion, anticipation and great enthusiasm to go after and get the goals I've set for that day and beyond.
7. I have learned some freeing things about fear. That fear is natural and inherent in me; that most fear I feel is evil and not even real; that real fear is present danger; and, last but not least, if whatever I am fearing is not a present dangerous threat, it is not real fear. Rather it is evil and irrational fear that I can cast down immediately with what is true.
8. I have learned that what it takes to start something is exactly what it will take to finish it. To persevere and focus until a project is finished. To keep the energy high and avoid going low at all costs because it takes way too much energy to go back up again.
9. I have learned to tell myself the truth when an unhealthy craving crops up. For example, the truth is, I do not want to eat because I am not truly scientifically hungry. The truth is, my spirit is what is craving and wants to be fed with that which truly satisfies.
10. I have learned that everything I say and do matters. That my daily disciplines are going to determine my destiny. How great (or not) the quality of my life is largely hinges on my routine day in and day out.

11. *I have learned to always seek ways to take myself to the next level. Constantly asking myself questions like, "how can I elevate? How can I go higher? What is the next level for me? What would it look like practically (in practice) for me to reach this next level?*
12. *I have learned there is nothing for me lying in bed snoozing. When I have gotten the adequate number of hours of sleep for my body to function well, snoozing over and over has zero benefit. It actually makes it more difficult to get up than when I first come to consciousness.*
13. *I have learned to focus on results. This simple shift in mindset has been pretty life-changing for me. To focus on results and not the pain of the process. Too often we dread something so much that it keeps us from taking care of business because it creates mental blocks among other self-sabotaging behavior such as procrastination.*
14. *I have learned that taking action is everything. Knowledge and wisdom must lead to action. If there is no action, there is no point in knowing.*
15. *I have learned that perfectionism is what kept me in a vicious cycle of stuckedness for well over a decade. Now I tell perfectionism where to go while I get to work creating as I was made to do. We are made to create and when we don't we exist in a perpetual state of frustration.*
16. *I have learned how to overcome fear. By realizing fear is evil deception that is overcome by knowing and operating in truth.*
17. *I have learned that hate, unforgiveness, bitterness and division has the power to make me physically sick. These ills cause dis-ease in the heart that cause disease in the body.*

18. *I have learned you will never really know how vital it is to move your body until you start moving your body. When you experience the vast mental and physical difference — for the better — in how you feel, you will testify to anyone who will listen that the human body is in fact made for moving most of the time. You will also wonder how you survived all those years of stasis.*

Appendix 5

Free Will Confession of Faith

As fate would have it, if you are reading this particular appendix, you are probably feeling a strong urge to put your faith in Jesus Christ. Sensing that doing so will be the mark of a new beginning for the person you know you are destined to be.

Because what I, Terri Andres, know for sure is this: our Father God desires to redeem your life from all pain and brokenness, and to set you completely free in a large place of healing, wholeness and abundance just as He redeemed my life 20-plus years ago and has set me in a large place of abundance in Him in every way.

Speaking out loud, make the following confession:

Father, I believe that Jesus Christ is your Son and Savior of the world. I believe Jesus came into the world, born of a virgin, and died on the cross for the forgiveness of my sins and redemption. I believe that Jesus Christ was buried and He defeated death because you Father God raised Him from the dead by the working of your mighty power.

Today, I confess Jesus Christ is Savior and Lord of all and I receive Him by faith as my personal Savior and Lord. Now, I am saved! I am born again. I am born of God.

Father fill me with Your Holy Spirit and baptize me with fire for supernatural power and ability to overcome every struggle within myself and my body so I can serve You and serve others.

By faith, I receive everything I have asked for. In the name of Jesus Christ. Hallelujah amen!

Appendix 6

Revelation and Notes

Use the following space to write down your important epiphanies/revelations and any other notes.

Acknowledgments

To the One I owe this abundant life I am living to. The victory song I sing incessantly is because you saw fit to rescue me from my self-destruction 20 some years ago when I didn't even have a clue as to who you were. My Christ.

To my mother, my doll. My angel. My best friend. My biggest fan. My cheerleader. My supporter. My encourager. My prayer partner and my example of grace, patience, humility and contentment. The one in this life who loves me with a love that I will never understand but will always strive to show my love, endless gratitude, appreciation and adoration that is beyond words.

To my father, my daddy. The man who created my physical being and gave me my name — which means brave harvester by the oath of God. The most chivalrous man I know who taught me the meaning of hard work and who continues to teach me so much about life, relationships, being an adult, being fearless, mentally tough, courageous and so much more. What an irreplaceable blessing you have been to me. That I get to say *I am a daddy's girl* is the sweetest thing.

To my other immediate, extended and spiritual family and friends. I am grateful to God to be connected to each of you in a significant way. I pray you personally know how much I appreciate you being a part of this life I am living.

To my Harvester team, I am so grateful for each and every one of you. Thank you for sharing and supporting our vision and mission with enthusiasm and zeal. Let's keep reaping from the great white harvest and light up the whole wide world for The One we love and serve. We are just getting started!

MEET THE AUTHOR

TERRI ANDRES is a woman of great passion, purpose and influence who has given her whole self and life to service. At the age of 23, she was radically saved and transformed into a brand new person through a supernatural encounter with God. Today, Terri is a formally trained minister in the Christian faith, a gifted communicator, leader, visionary, entrepreneur and philanthropist. When she is not working, she is resting and enjoying life with her loved ones.

www.ingramcontent.com/pod-product-compliance
Lightning Source LLC
Chambersburg PA
CBHW011147290426
44109CB00023B/2520